THE

LIVERPO[OL]

INCLU[DING]

SKETCH OF THE ENVIRONS:

WITH A

MAP OF THE TOWN.

By W. MOSS.

THE SECOND EDITION, ENLARGED.

LIVERPOOL:

PRINTED BY T. SWARBRECK,
FOR W. JONES, BOOKSELLER, CASTLE-STREET; AND
SOLD BY VERNOR AND HOOD, LONDON.

1797.

Aug.ᵗ 10ᵗʰ 1798; Wilkinson Sept.ʳ 9ᵗʰ 1809

T O

THE RIGHT HONOURABLE

THE *EARL* OF *LIVERPOOL*;

WHOSE ABILITIES AND EXERTIONS HAVE SO EMI-
NENTLY CONTRIBUTED TO THE

COMMERCIAL INTERESTS OF THE NATION,

AND OF WHICH

L I V E R P O O L

HAS SO AMPLY PARTICIPATED;

THIS SKETCH

OF THE GROWING PROSPERITY OF A TOWN SO APPRO-
PRIATELY DISTINGUISHED

BY HIS ADOPTION,

IS,

WITH THE HIGHEST RESPECT,

INSCRIBED BY

LIVERPOOL,
21ST AUGUST 1797.   THE AUTHOR.

THE FIRST LIVERPOOL GUIDE BOOK
BY W. MOSS, 1797

with additional material by
David Brazendale

Palatine Books, 2007

New text copyright © David Brazendale, 2007

First published in 2007 by Palatine Books,
an imprint of Carnegie Publishing
Carnegie House, Chatsworth Road, Lancaster LA1 4SL
www.palatinebooks.com

ISBN 978-1-874181-46-0

British Library Cataloguing-in-Publication data
A catalogue record for this book is available from the British Library

Designed and typeset by Carnegie Book Production, Lancaster
Printed and bound by Alden Press, Oxford

This book is for the members of my immediate family
Liz and Andy, Richard and Fiona
and the 'Famous Five'
Luke, Matthew, James, Jonathan and Joseph

That they may understand something of Liverpool's past.

View of Liverpool from Tranmere, 1795

In this view the town's principal churches – St Nicholas, St Peter's and
St George's – can be identified, together with the dome of the Town Hall. The
ship firing a salute to the consternation of the observers is probably a naval
frigate. In the autumn of 1799, just four years after this illustration was drawn,
a ship decided to announce its arrival: 'unknown to the gunner, the ball had not
been withdrawn. The shot entered the town near the south end of the dry dock,
carried off the arm of a cooper … passing the corner of the Old Dock, it killed
William Treasure the mate of the ship *William* and another man, a roper …
who was standing at the bottom of Hanover Street … [it] … struck the corner
of a house, and '… severely wounded another man. Since this accident no ship
has been allowed to salute the town, under a penalty of £10'.
(Lacey's *Stranger in Liverpool*)

Preface

This new edition of Moss' *Guide Book to Liverpool* has its origins in a copy inherited from my grandfather – a keen student of Liverpool's past. Liverpool has attracted interest, praise and condemnation in almost equal measure over the past three hundred years. At this time of the double celebration of the eight hundredth anniversary, in 2007, of the grant of borough status by King John, and its year of European prominence as the Capital of Culture it seemed appropriate that the views, thoughts and perspectives of the first writer to provide insights for strangers into the town should be made available once more.

This new edition is illustrated with a selection of paintings, drawings, engravings and lithographs dating from the period during which Moss was writing. Some of these works are previously unpublished, but all have come from the splendid collections held by the Athenaeum, an institution which Moss would have known and which in its origins and intent clearly reflects the view of their city and of themselves taken by the new middle class of the emerging metropolis. I must express my deep appreciation of the way in which the President and Proprietors of the Athenaeum have made their resources available to me. I am also grateful to the President and Council of the Historic Society of Lancashire and Cheshire who have enabled me to make use of material from their proceedings.

The short notes on various aspects of life in Liverpool in the period are intended to illuminate and enlarge on what Moss writes or questions he raises. Additionally, it is hoped that the bibliography will direct the reader who wishes to know more to at least one source which may be found helpful.

As always a book is not the product of one person and at all stages I have received support, help and encouragement from numerous people. As always, I acknowledge my debt in this as in so much else to my wife, Hilary, without her help, support and input it could never have been done. Alistair Hodge and Judith Franks of Carnegie Publishing have not only encouraged the project, and taken the photographs but also guided me through the publishing minefield. The Chairman of the Library Committee of the Athenaeum, Mr John Tiernan and the librarians, Mr V. Roper and Ms P. Keen, have always been patient and helpful as have the staff of libraries in Sefton and the University of Liverpool. My friend, Len Fender has used his skills to take some of the photographs and for this I am very grateful.

No book has ever been written which does not contain errors of fact and judgement; for any that appear here I take full responsibility.

David Brazendale

Abbreviations

THLC	Transactions of the Historic Society of Lancashire and Cheshire
RLC	Record Society of Lancashire and Cheshire
Chet.Soc.	Publications of the Chetham Society. These have been published in three series, indicated by o.s. (Old Series), n.s. (New Series) and 3rd s. (Third Series).
RCHM	Royal Commission on Historic Monuments

Eighteenth-century guide books

The original 'tourists' were the sons of noble families who, during the seventeenth and eighteenth centuries, were sent on the 'Grand Tour', a cultural journey undertaken mainly in Italy, though sometimes including the towns of France or Austria. To guide them, to make sure that they saw the best sites, monuments, collections and galleries and also to ensure that they absorbed the language and culture of the countries they visited, they were accompanied by a tutor who had studied the art, history and architecture of the places on the itinerary.

By the last decades of the eighteenth century, people of more humble social status were beginning to find their way to the Continent. Unable to afford the services of a tutor, the cicerone,* and a train of servants they sought information about their destinations in a new literary genre. These books, intended to guide the discerning visitor, were a development of the eighteenth century and were to reach their height of popularity in the nineteenth and twentieth centuries, when earnest tourists, anxious to improve their minds, poring earnestly over their Baedeker volume (first published in 1827) made sure that they saw all that was remarkable or worthy in the towns they visited. Improvements in transport and the growth of a monied middle class caused a rapid expansion of tourism and these intrepid travellers were determined to expand their horizons and broaden their experience. However, people were moving not just for pleasure or instruction but in the course of business and commerce. It was primarily this type of person to whom the first *Liverpool Guide* was directed.

---

* 'cicerone', a guide, one who conducts visitors and sightseers to museums, galleries, etc., and explains matters of historic or artistic interest.

Dr William Moss, a surgeon and man-midwife of the Dispensary, had first begun to reveal the glories of Liverpool in his medical survey of the town in the 1780s. He soon realised that a new type of visitor would be coming to Liverpool and that this vibrant, prosperous, rapidly expanding town would attract those who came in the furtherance of trade. He also believed that the town would attract the curious, anxious to see this prodigy of the modern world at first hand. Additionally, the area had all the qualifications to attract those seeking the fashionable cure of sea bathing (clean waters, wide sands and lodging houses), added to which was the excitement of a great commercial harbour with a plethora of vessels to enliven the scene. For those sated with the pleasures of the seashore there were pleasant walks and excursions to be enjoyed.

Moss was also filled with a sense of civic pride, and gloried in the fantastic advances made by his home town. He was inspired to draw the attention of visitors to the achievements of the authorities and its go-getting inhabitants who were so busy carving out new trades, new trade routes and developing what was soon to be recognised as the second port and city of the kingdom. He was not quite the first to pioneer a guide to Liverpool. In 1795 Henry Wallace had published what he intended as an academic history of the town. He explored the origins of the place name; he described climate and geology; he studied the demography of the rapidly expanding population; and he measured the streets and buildings. He also outlined the system of government, and the huge expansion in trade and commerce, and when all this was done he began a description of the town and its buildings. It was not truly a guide book, but it did set the pattern for the books which were to follow it. Moss, to some extent, followed this precedent but brought to it his own perceptions, preoccupations and interests. One of the most refreshing features of Moss's *Liverpool Guide* of 1797 is the way in which the man and his character permeate what might often have been a dull recital of facts and statistics.

Dr William Moss

The medical fraternity of Liverpool, in the second half of the
eighteenth century, were an important and influential group in the
town which was well served by its doctors. In 1744 the Mayor, himself
a surgeon, and a number of other prominent citizens, had opened a
fund for the provision of an Infirmary in the town. The building was
completed and opened in 1749 near the present day site of St George's
Hall. The Infirmary was limited to treating subscribers and those whom
they nominated, provided that they were not a pregnant woman, under
seven years of age, did not need an operation or were 'disordered
in their senses'. In 1778, many of the Liverpool doctors contributed
to the establishment of the Dispensary, located in Church Street.
The purpose of this facility was to provide outpatient advice and the
prescription and dispensing of medicines. The Dispensary also housed
the medical library, which had been set up in 1779 by a group of the
local doctors to provide a place of study and reference.

Dr Moss was on the staff of the Dispensary. He was a keen
student of obstetrics and among his responsibilities was the supervision
and training of the midwives, who were appointed by the Vestry from
1790. From its foundation in 1793, he was a staunch supporter of the
Ladies Charity which undertook the care of impoverished pregnant
women. However, Moss was more than a surgeon and accoucher
(professions both rather despised at the time). He was a scholar and,
in addition to the *Guide*, wrote a number of works. In 1781 he wrote
An Essay on the Management and Nursing of Children which was an
intelligent and comprehensive guide to the birth, upbringing and health
of children. This was followed, in 1784, by *A Familiar Medical Survey
of Liverpool* from which he quotes extensively in the guide book. He
waxes lyrical on the fresh air and free play of the winds in Liverpool
and even the fumes from the copperas [sulphuric acid] works, the

stench of tar and pitch, the reek of tobacco factories and the oil house are all, according to him, beneficial to health. Even the thick clouds of coal smoke which enveloped the town were only detrimental to 'the chesty subject'. In Moss' mind only the smells of the slaughter houses and the salt house were likely to be dangerous.

Medical men of the period were obsessed with drainage, fresh air, ventilation and 'effluvia'. The mechanism for the generation and spread of infection was a medical mystery but the theory most favoured was the malign influence of the effluvia or miasmas of dirt and stagnant water, hence the emphasis, often to be detected, on good drainage and the beneficial effects of sandy or gravel soil. As Moss writes 'If we examine the surrounding countryside [of Liverpool] we shall find it every where, ... free from morass, stagnant water, wood or any other cause or causes that can in any material degree conspire against, ... the human constitution. The soil is sandy; which promotes the ready absorption, ... which contributes essentially to the health of the town.' In this medical elysium, he says 'infectious fevers seldom obtain a hold, agues (malarial fevers) are seldom experienced and kidney stones are rare'.

It must be said that Moss recognised the danger to health in the overcrowding of dark, damp dwellings, lacking even the most basic sanitary facilities; especially unhealthy was the use of cellar dwellings. These became very prevalent as poor labourers flocked into the city to supply the constant demand for manual workers. His rose-tinted view of the medical climate of Liverpool was clouded by the fact that the expectation of life for working class men in the town was twenty years.

By the time of Moss' death in 1802, Liverpool, with its hospitals and successful doctors, was well on the way to establishing its reputation as place of medical excellence.

Contents

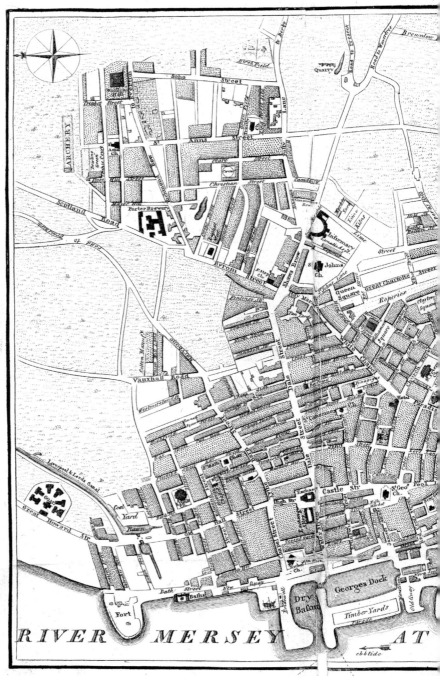

RIVER MERSEY AT

Published as the Act directs Feb.ᵞ 1ˢᵗ 17

Seacome Ferry   odside Ferry

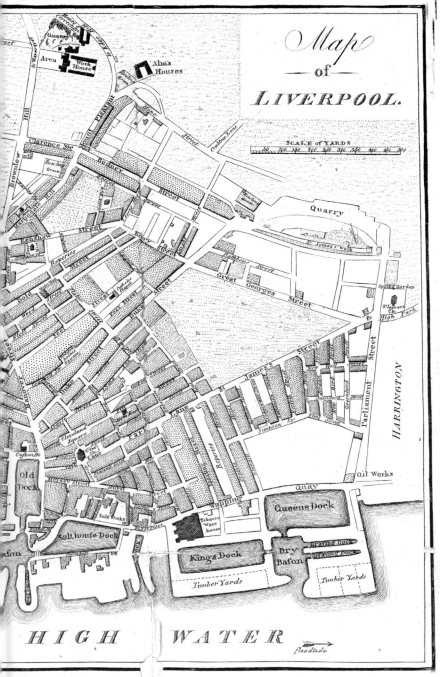

Map
—of—
LIVERPOOL.

SCALE of YARDS

Quarry

St James's Walk

Spring Garden
St James's Ch.
High Park

HARRINGTON

Great Georges Street

Parliament Street

James's Street

Oil Works

Quay

Queens Dock

Salt Works

Salthouse Dock

Tobacco Ware house

King's Dock

Dry Bason

Graving Dock

Timber Yards

Timber Yards

Old Dock

Custom Ho

Cleveland Square

Bason

HIGH WATER floodtide →

by WILLIAM JONES. astle Street.

THE LIVERPOOL GUIDE

L IVERPOOL being the first town in the kingdom in point
of *size and commercial importance,** the metropolis excepted,
has of late been the resort of a great number of visitors, for the
purposes of commerce.

The advantages the town possesses in its near connexion
and ready communication, by internal rivers and canals, with
the extensive manufacturing town and neighbourhoods of
Manchester; the coal country of Wigan: the unrivalled potteries of
Staffordshire; the exclusive export of Salt; its central situation on
the western coast of the kingdom, thereby communicating readily
with Dublin and the northern parts of Ireland; and finally, the
goodness of the Harbour and the very superior accommodation
for Shipping; have all conspired to form it into a vortex that has
nearly swallowed up the foreign trade of Bristol, Lancaster, and
Whitehaven.

Wealth being the result of commerce, the flourishing state
of the town has enabled it to make efforts for its internal
improvement, and which it has recently done in a manner not a
little extraordinary; this, with the pleasant and salubrious situation
of the town, the convenience of sea bathing, its amusements, and
the lively cheerful air which regularly pervades it, have of late
years made it the resort also of *strangers* of all descriptions, for the
purposes of health and amusement; and have made it necessary to
procure a GUIDE to direct them to, and explain such objects as
may be most worthy their attention.

---

* These circumstances will be explained in their proper places.

They who would wish to inform themselves more particularly of the history of the town, its increase of trade and population, and the comparative salubrity of its situation, may, at their leisure, consult the following publications, being all that have appeared on those subjects:

"An *Essay* towards the *History of Liverpool*, by W. ENFIELD; with *Views* of the *Public Structures*, a *Chart* of the *Harbour*, and a *Map* of the *Environs.*" – Folio, 1773.

"A *Familiar Medical Survey* of *Liverpool*; addressed to the *Inhabitants*. Containing *Observations* on the *Situation* of the *Town*, the *Qualities* and *Influence* of the *Air*, the *Employments* and *Manner* of *Living* of the *Inhabitants*, &c. By W. MOSS, *Surgeon*, LIVERPOOL.*" – Small Octavo, 1784.

"A *General* and *Descriptive History* of the ancient and present *State* of the *Town* of *Liverpool*, &c." – Octavo, 1795. No AUTHOR'S name.

"*The Liverpool Directory*, by J. GORE," 1796.

DR. AIKEN'S "*Description* of the *Country* round *Manchester*," gives a detail of the history and commerce of Liverpool; 4to, 1796.

INNS AND TAVERNS.

The Inns are numerous, and equally variable in their accommodations, adapted to all rank and descriptions of travellers.

The largest Inn is the *Hotel* at the bottom of Lord-street; where are accommodations for families of the first rank, their retinues, carriages, and horses; as also every other description of travellers, who wish to be well accommodated. There is a public ordinary every day.

This situation is deemed the most central in the town; it is also the lowest with respect to elevation.

The next, in point of magnitude, is the *King's Arms*, in Water-street, near the Exchange; and furnishes accommodations nearly as extensive as the Hotel, either for parties, families, or single travellers. It has a public ordinary. It was formerly the successive residence of some of the most distinguished merchants of Liverpool.

Immediately adjoining the King's Arms, is the *Talbot Inn and London Tavern*; and which is very similar, in accommodation, to the former. The Mail and other London coaches put up there. It is much frequented by travellers to and from Dublin. A public ordinary.

The *Crown Inn*, Redcross-street; a commodious house. London and other stage coaches go from hence.

The *Golden Lion*, top of Dale-street; formerly the largest and best Inn in the town, consequently has many accommodations for travellers. Some of the Warrington, Manchester, &c. stage coaches, go from hence. A public ordinary.

The *Angel Inn*, a little lower down in Dale-street; a commodious travellers Inn. Stage coaches for Warrington, Manchester, &c. likewise go from this house. A public ordinary.

There are other travellers and carriers Inns in Dale-street, High-street, Tythebarn-street, &c.

The GOLDEN LION INN, & the Old Public House adjoining, Dale Street.
1828.

THE ANGEL INN, Dale Street, 1830.

Liverpool Inns

It was in Dale Street that the greatest number of the better hotels, inns and
taverns of Liverpool were to be found, though Dr Moss gives a great boost to
the Hotel, located in Lord Street. These drawings by a Liverpool drawing master
James Brierley, are taken from a large collection of similar ink and wash drawings
of buildings, streets and churches held by the Athenaeum. They emphasise that
even in 1830 the street architecture of Liverpool was varied and irregular.

The *Star and Garter*, Paradise-street; a Tavern, not an Inn.
Genteel accommodations for parties, for eating or lodging, upon
the plan of a regular Tavern.

The *Globe Tavern*, John-street; similar to the Star and Garter.
A public ordinary.*

The wines are in general of a good quality at the principal
Inns and Taverns, from the opportunities the keepers have of
purchasing them in their pure state, on their immediate landing
upon the quays, from abroad.

---

* Private lodgings may always be had, and frequently ready furnished houses, by
application at the Inns and Taverns.

The Development of Liverpool, 1660–1800

In 1698, Celia Fiennes described Liverpool as 'A very rich trading town … it is London in miniature as much as ever I saw anything'. In the same decade Daniel Defoe referred to the town as 'a large, handsome, well built and increasing town'. Locals, too, were astonished at the rapid growth of Liverpool from an insignificant port and market. William Blundell, squire of Little Crosby, who had profited from investment in Liverpool's expanding trade, wrote 'The buildings and people of Liverpool; our next post town, are certainly more than doubly augmented and the custom [port revenue] eight or ten fold increased within the twenty eight years last past' . He was writing, in 1693, at the request of a London publisher who had asked for information on local wonders for inclusion in a new edition of Camden's *Britannia*. Blundell's note firmly sets the time frame for Liverpool's expansion into an international trading port and metropolis in the years after the Restoration.

The period between 1660 and 1690 saw a worldwide expansion in British trade which was reaching every known continent. Much of this growth was on the Atlantic seaboard, along the coast of Africa, to the new colonies in North America and the West Indies and the Spanish Main. New commodities, tobacco, sugar, rum, dyewoods and products such as rice and indigo were being imported to Britain. It has been suggested that the disasters of pestilence and fire in London, in 1665 and 1666 drove merchants to seek new commercial opportunities elsewhere. Liverpool's first sugar refinery was established by just such a man in 1666.

Previously, the ports of southern England had been the main centres of maritime activity. In the new Atlantic trade, voyages from west coast ports, such as Bristol and Liverpool, benefited from the shorter distances involved. In the period 1660–1800, when Britain was involved in almost continuous warfare with continental powers, notably Spain, the Netherlands and France, the activities of enemy warships and privateers made the English Channel highly dangerous. Ships using Liverpool or other western ports could avoid the perilous waters of the narrow seas. Another advantage enjoyed by Liverpool was that the town was unrestricted by ancient practices and regulations which made it, though difficult to navigate, an attractive and economical harbour.

Liverpool was not only concerned with a growing trade to the

Americas. There was also increased contact with the ports of the Mediterranean for the import of wine and fruit (a cargo of Spanish oranges entered the Mersey in Elizabethan times). Liverpool was at the centre of trade with Ireland and the Isle of Man. Coal, iron, textiles, and pottery, produced in the adjacent towns of Prescot and Rainford, were exported in return for cattle, wool and linen. Lancashire's development as an industrial area led to Liverpool becoming the focus of a highly profitable trade. This involved the refining of salt, brought down the River Weaver Navigation (opened 1732) from the salt fields of Cheshire, and processed, mainly in Liverpool, using coal from the St Helens' coalfield, which after 1757 was carried down the Sankey Brook navigation (St Helens Canal). This trade has been claimed, by some historians, to have made a greater contribution to the prosperity of Liverpool than the infamous slave trade.

Two sets of statistics give a clear picture of Liverpool's growth. In 1715, 17,780 tons of cargo entered the port of Liverpool, with exports of 18,400 tons. By the mid-century traffic had grown to 31,731 tons inwards and 33,693 tons outward; by 1800 a figure of some 400,000 tons had been achieved, in terms of both import and export trade. The town experienced a comparable growth in population, estimated at 7,000 in 1700: by 1773 it had reached 34,407 and by 1800 was 83,708. This increase was only achieved by massive inward migration from the surrounding countryside, Wales and to a limited extent from Ireland (the days of the Irish influx were yet to come). These arrivals offset the ever rising mortality of the slums that were springing up along the streets described by Moss.

IRISH, &c. PACKETS.

There are several packets to Dublin, for the express purpose of conveying passengers, horses, carriages and luggage only; all of which are very commodious, and sail almost daily, when the wind permits. For particulars, the stranger will be conducted to the different packet-offices for information. There are a number of trading vessels to Dublin and all parts of Ireland, particularly to the northern ports.

There are a few packets to the Isle of Man, of similar construction and convenience with those to Dublin.

FERRY BOATS.

These are numerous across the river into *Cheshire*, to the different ferry-houses. It is to be regretted, that, as at most ferrys, the prices and other regulations should not be fixed, so as to be under the control of the magistrate, as on the Thames; which would prevent the daily impositions that are practised, especially upon strangers, and which are frequently to a shameful excess.

The ferry-houses on the opposite shore in Cheshire, are (beginning with the lowest down the river, northward, and continuing in succession southward, up the river) *Seacombe, Woodside, Rock House, New Ferry, Eastham,* and the *Chester Canal Boat House.* The first four are navigated by open boats of different sizes, for the conveyance of passengers, horses, carriages, cattle, &c. All, except the first and last, communicate with Chester by good roads, post chaise, &c. The first has a chaise to the Hotel at Highlake; and the last communicates with Chester by an elegant packet on the Canal. Beside post chaise, there is a double stage coach from Eastham to Chester. Passengers to Eastham and the Canal, are conveyed in large covered boats, that are very commodious, as they each contain two distinct cabins, and do not carry horses, &c.

The fare from hence to Eastham and Chester in the first apartments, is 3*s*. In the second 1*s*. 8*d*. without any other expence. From hence to the Canal Boat; the first cabin 1*s*. the second 6*d*. the Canal Boat, first cabin 1*s*. the second 6*d*. the whole 2*s*. 6*d*. and 1*s*. 6*d*.

The fare to the first four Ferrys, is twopence for market people and common passengers. Sixpence is generally expected from the upper orders of passengers. A boat for one person across the river is commonly 1*s*. two or more may be conveyed for the same price. A party of more than two may hire a boat for 2*s*. to take them over, and bring them back at any time they please, that the wind and weather will permit; being careful to make an agreement beforehand, and not to pay till their return; otherwise imposition would be the certain consequence. The smaller boats with one mast each, are to be preferred, in moderate weather, to the larger with two; as they are handier, can land in shallower water, are capable of being rowed in calms or contrary winds, and are equally safe. The passengers of both sexes are carried in and out of the boats by the boat-men, with great ease and safety, when the tide will not allow of their approaching sufficiently near the piers.*

HACKNEY COACHES AND CHAIRS.

Hackney coaches, are numerous; and may be had, at any time, to any part of the town and country, except, as in London, on the, sudden fall of rain. The fares and regulations, very similar to those in London, are as follow:

FARES OF COACHES AND CHAIRS IN TOWN.

For carrying four passengers, not exceeding a mile 1 6
For carrying four passengers above a mile, and not exceeding a
    mile and a half 1 6
And in like proportion for a greater distance.
If required to go out of the direct way to set down any person,
    the further sum of 0 6
And if required to take in other passengers before the end of the
    fare (the whole not exceeding four) for each such detention, the
    further sum of 0 6
For a coach and pair, carrying four passengers per day . . . 12 6
For the same per hour, the first 1 6
Each successive one 1 3
NOTE – *It shall be at the Coachman's option to go by time or distance.*
If he go by distance, and be required to stop and wait, he is to
    have, for every quarter of an hour's waiting 0 6
When called from home after twelve at night, double fare, except
    on assembly, play, or public concert nights, when double fare
    shall not be paid till one in the morning.
All distances to be measured the nearest carriage way from the
    place the person is first taken up at.

---

* This awkward practice prevails chiefly on the opposite shore; the projecting *pier* and *slip* at St George's dock, which extend to low water mark, prevent the necessity of it *there*.

RULES FOR THE REGULATION OF COACHMEN.

1. Every coach shall be numbered and entered at the Town Clerk's office. – Penalty, 10s.
2. No coachmen shall demand more than the rates before allowed, or refuse or delay to drive a fare for the same, when called, by day or night, fair or foul weather. – Penalty, 10s.
3. No coachman shall refuse the first fare that offers, unless really pre-engaged. – Penalty, 10s.
4. Every coachman shall have a check-string, from the inside of his carriage, fastened round his hand or arm, when driving a fare. – Penalty, 5s.
5. No coachman shall leave his carriage, or suffer it to stand in any street or thoroughfare by night. – Penalty, 10s.
6. No coachman shall drive his carriage upon the foot-way in any street or high road. – Penalty, 10s.
7. Every person calling a coach, and not employing it according to the call, shall pay the coachman half (and if kept waiting fifteen minutes or more, the whole) of the intended fare. – Penalty, 10s.
8. No person shall blot out, deface, or alter the number of any coach. – Penalty, 10s.

CHAIRS.

Any distance under 1000 yards 0 6
Above 1000 yards, and not more than a mile. 1 0
And in proportion for greater distances.
Chairmen shall wait or stop five minutes at a time, or fifteen minutes in the whole, of one fare; but if detained longer, and not more than half an hour, they receive, beside the fare . 0 6
Chairmen are under the same regulations as Coachmen.
Complaints for both to be preferred to the Mayor or other Magistrate of the town, within six days; the fines to be divided between the informer and the poor.

SURVEY OF THE TOWN, DOCKS, &c.[*]

The stranger, in viewing the town to the best advantage, should begin at the EXCHANGE; where the spacious street before him;[†] perfectly uniform on the right hand, and nearly so on the left; all shops, containing every thing useful and ornamental, to indulge the taste and gratify the necessities; presents a view not to be excelled, perhaps in the *Capital*. The *spire* of *St. George's Church*, on the right, shooting over the lofty buildings near the middle of the street, which is terminated by the beautiful eastern extremity of the Church, and the perspective finished by the distant appearance of ships masts; with the extreme point of *St. Thomas's* spire, on the left; affords a view as grand as it is novel. To the right, in the middle of Castle-street, *Brunswick-street* affords a view of the ships in *St. George's* Dock.

Around the Church, is the market for vegetables and fruit. Vegetables, the growth of the open garden, are found here earlier, in greater perfection and abundance, and cheaper, than in any other part of the kingdom. Oranges, from Spain, Portugal, and the Western Islands, in the season, are commonly so plentiful, as to scent the ambient air as fully as when in their native groves. The surrounding country being unfavourable to the production of the more delicate fruits, they are not very plentiful here. The best may be had in the shops on the east side of Castle-street, already passed. In turning about, when at the church, the reverse view of Castle-street is, of course, obtained, and which is terminated by the front of the Exchange; except that, at the opening on the right of the Exchange, *St. Paul's* may be seen, at a distance, to raise its swelling dome above the interposing buildings, and to

---

[*] The following *survey* may be made in a carriage, on horse-back, or on foot, as the weather and other circumstances favour it. In wet weather, the neighbourhoods of the docks are generally too dirty, for ladies especially, to walk; and therefore the *accompaniment* of a carriage, &c. may be necessary; but less so from that cause in dry weather. The length of this first part of the ramble, is about three miles; but which the varying amusements appear to shorten.

[†] Castle-street; the *Cheapside* of Liverpool.

M. A. Rooker delin.　　　　　　　　　　　　　　*Edw.ᵈ Rooker sculp.*

S.ᵗ Georges Church.

finish the view. This dome will be seen more perfectly, when some houses are taken down to widen the street beyond the Exchange. The Exchange also will be more perfect when the intended cupola is erected; and more especially if its mountainous roof, at present so offensive to the eye, should be removed.

Castle-street being wider at the north than the south end; it was proposed to bring the east side forward, for the purpose

Drawn by W.H.Watt.   *Engraved by W.m. Green.*

A View of Castle Street in

View of Castle Street

This view is dated *c.* 1770 and shows Castle Street and St George's church
as Dr Moss would have known them. The site of the church had formerly
been occupied by the castle, which after the Civil War had been abandoned
and allowed to fall into total decrepitude. The ruins were acquired by the
Corporation in 1707 and the buildings demolished by *c.* 1720. St George's
church, designed by Thomas Steers, was built on the site. This church became
the civic church and was attended by the Mayor, aldermen and common council
men as well as those anxious to rise in the town's hierarchy. These included, for
a time, the great evangelical and hymn writer, John Newton, Customs Collector
for the port. The area around the church was a fruit market – the two, domed
pavilions were used by the market officers and one may have served as a lock-up.

of obtaining a regular perspective, and by which means the
Exchange would finally have terminated the view on the east as
it now does on the west side of the street. Mr. WYATT, the
architect, being consulted, gave it as his opinion, that it would
be better to let it remain as it is. A little irregularity in a view is
often more pleasing than studied uniformity; and which appears

to be the case in that before us. This street was so called from a
castle, which once stood where we now are. It was surrounded by
a ditch twelve yards wide and ten deep; communicating with the
river by a covered way, which yet remains. It was otherwise well
fortified; as, in 1644, the Parliament forces sustained a siege of
a month, under the command of Colonel More, against Prince
Rupert, before it was taken.

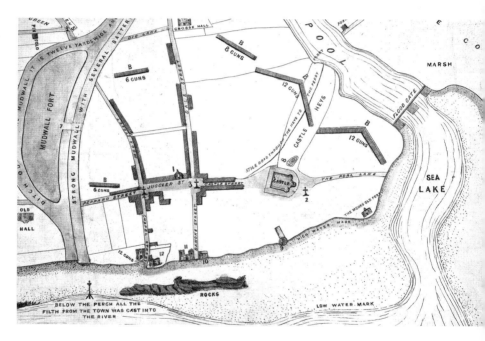

This is a nineteenth-century map, based on scanty written sources and some
conjecture, of the defences of Liverpool during its time of parliamentarian
occupation in 1644. The town was stormed by the troops of Prince Rupert's
army on the night of 12 June 1644. An eyewitness writes, 'Prince Rupert's men,
upon their first entrance, did ... slay almost all they met with, to the number of
three hundred and sixty, and among them others, diverse of their own friends
and artificers, that never bore armes in their lives, yea, even one poore blind
man.' (*Life of Adam Martindale*, Chetham Soc., os, vol. 4 (1845)). Apart from the
military details this map gives useful topographical insights into the town and
shows the line of the Pool and its feeder stream, mentioned in Moss' text as
being the line of Whitechapel and Paradise Street.

Pursuing the course down *Pool-lane,* the eye should not
be turned to either side, as it would be offended at the very
indecorous practice of exposing the shambles meat in the public

Widening of Castle Street at Preeson's Row drawn by Matthew Gregson

The Liverpool Improvement Act of 1786 gave the Corporation powers to widen
and pave streets. Castle Street, as one of the principal thoroughfares and in
close proximity to the Exchange, was one of the first to be improved. The
original intention was to shift the axis of the street to allow the Town Hall
a central position. Many alleys and ramshackle buildings were cleared away,
amongst them Gregson's own shop, to create the handsome street which exists
today. Though many of the new Georgian buildings have been replaced, traces
of them can still be seen on the upper floors of some shops on the western side.
An interesting survival is a stone embedded in the roadway at the north end of
the street. This is the remaining marker stone of the area in which the annual
fair, instituted in 1292, was held. Those trading were immune from arrest for
debt, and consequently it is known as the sanctuary stone.

The Old Dock, 1799

This drawing gives a clear impression of how the construction of the dock had facilitated the handling of cargo, with the wagons and carts able to be drawn up on a level with the ship's deck. It will be observed that at this time the dock was not enclosed or protected in any way. Later, posts and chains were introduced to prevent 'strangers and others falling in, in the night, from missing their way, from intoxication etc.' The red brick building on the left, flying the Union flag, is the custom house. This replaced the older building at the foot of Water Street and was part of the development of the Pool area when the dock was built. It was ornamented with a carved royal arms and enclosed a yard and warehouse. The warehouses on the south side of the dock were also part of the development of this area by the Corporation.

street,* but be directed straight forward to the ships, which will be found to be in the *Old Dock*, at the bottom of the street.† The view backward, from the bottom of this street, has a good effect.

---

* An Act of Parliament was obtained, some years ago, to suppress this custom, and remove the slaughterhouses, but has not yet been put in force.

† The shambles, however, are confined to the upper part of the street, and some good shops will be found lower down.

Liverpool's Dock Development I

Though Liverpool's central position on the west coast gave it certain advantages, the harbour itself had a number of deficiencies and difficulties of navigation that had to be overcome before the town could develop into a world, oceanic port.

The original site of the town was on a peninsula, running along a northwest–southeast axis. To the west lay the Mersey while the eastern flank was washed by the waters of the Pool. The latter was the estuary of a stream which rose near the present site of the University of Liverpool, flowed down the hill and then along the line of Bryom Street, Whitechapel and Paradise Street to emerge into the Mersey at Canning Place. The estuary of the Pool was wide, shallow and silted and at low tide the mud banks were exposed. The Pool provided shelter for the small fishing and coastal vessels that plied a trade around the shores of the Celtic Sea.

The Mersey shoreline, still marked today by the road named the Strand, was also used for the lading and discharge of cargo from ships but was more exposed to the rigours of wind and tide. Ships were grounded on the sands, though the hazards of outcrops of rock near St Nicholas Church and the dumps of shingle ballast left by previous occupants of the berth were an ever-present danger. The handling of ships on the river and those beached on the Strand was made more difficult by the wide tidal range. The Mersey estuary has one of the greatest tidal ranges of any port in Britain and water levels can rise and fall by over 30 feet (10 metres). The effect of the tide is exacerbated by the bottle shape of the estuary which ensures that, at the ebb, the waters accumulated in the broad reaches east of Liverpool pour through the narrows opposite the town. This tide race plays a part in sluicing sand from the channel but can make navigation difficult and dangerous.

As the ships became bigger and designed for deep water sailing, the cargo handling facilities at Liverpool proved inadequate. Development of the harbour in its early days is obscure. A quay had been built at the foot of Water Street, its date is not recorded but it was in existence by 1546. This feature gave its name to the chapel which was dedicated to St Mary del Key (quay). The first evidence of attempts to improve the harbour comes in 1635 when a proposal by the

Corporation for the construction of a quay and harbour was discussed but set aside. However, the next year, a quay was ordered to be built, under the supervision of a team of four mariners, on the bank of the Pool, overlooked by the dilapidated remains of the castle. Another device used for the improvement of the Pool was the construction of a sluice gate, where the stream entered the estuary, to allow for scouring the basin of sand and mud at low tide.

By the last decades of the seventeenth century the increased trade and the enlargement of ships using the port required drastic action. In 1696 Granville Collins in his 'Coasting Pilot' wrote 'The ships lye aground before the town of Liverpool; tis bad riding afloat by reason of the strong tydes that run here, therefore ships that ride afloat, ride up the Slyne where the tide is less'. The Slyne or Sloyne is the broader

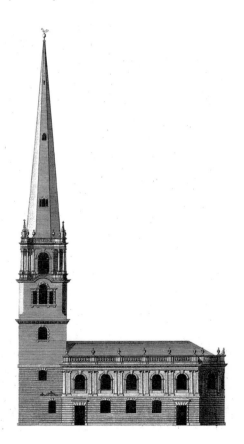

St Thomas' church

This church in Frederick Street was the fourth church in Liverpool and was built between 1748 and 1750 as the town expanded beyond the former Pool. The architect of the classical building was Henry Sephton, who was a prominent local mason and builder at this time. The body of the church was built of stone with Ionic pilasters and decorated with cornices and balustrades. The most notable feature of the church was its tall, elegant spire of 216 feet. In 1757 a hurricane blew down over forty feet of the spire. When rebuilt it was lowered by eighteen feet but remained unstable until its eventual demolition in 1822 'to prevent mischief'.

stretch of the river off Rock Ferry above the narrowest channel. When ships lay off in the river, the cargo had to be carried ashore in lighters and boats, with a consequent increase of costs and danger of damage.

These problems exercised the minds of the wealthy merchants and there seem to have been discussions about the possibility of enhancing the port's provision in the last decades of the seventeenth century. The town's new charter of 1695 put civic control in the hands of a mercantile elite, anxious to develop trade. Added immediacy was given when, in 1703, the shipping in the river was devastated by the Great Hurricane. The same storm which destroyed the first Eddystone lighthouse and the fleet of Sir Cloudesley Shovel on its return to England from the Mediterranean.

This was the first made dock in Liverpool, about 75 years ago. Its scite [*sic*] was a *Pool*, that wound and extended the whole length of the old and high part of the town, on the east side, along Paradise-street and Whitechapel. Tradition says, that a singular bird, called a *Liver*, formerly frequented this *pool*; hence the place was called *Liverpool*, and the *Liver* adopted as its *Crest*.

The first idea that strikes a stranger, on coming to this dock, is the singularity of so great a number of ships in the *heart of the town*, without discovering any communication with the *sea*. He must awhile suspend his curiosity, and turn to the left. Viewing the commodious lading and unlading of the ships, as he proceeds along the quay, till he has turned the first corner of the dock; he will there be presented with a view of the *Custom House*, on the left, and the beautiful spire of *St. Thomas's Church*, rising majestically before him over the buildings which terminates his view in front.

Chains will be found to extend along the dock; which became necessary to prevent strangers and others falling in in the night, from missing their way, from intoxication, &c.

Proceeding still along the quay, the Custom House is passed; which has nothing, external, to recommend it to an particular notice. Its situation is central with respect to the docks, and therefore commodious. – Near this south east corner of the dock, are extensive warehouses of the various productions of the Staffordshire potteries.

Pursuing this direction, without turning the next corner of the dock, which would afford nothing new,* an opening presents into *Clieveland-square*. The *obelisk* in the centre, the original attempt at uniformity in the buildings, with the once row of trees before the houses, conspired to make it an eligible residence. It has ceased to be so now, as may be observed from the almost total loss of the trees, houses being made into shops, and the square being converted into a market of all sorts of provisions and wares.† This square terminates at the opposite extremity with a street called *Pitt-street*, so named after the father of the present Chancellor of the Exchequer.

Two Duke Street Residents

If Dr Moss, as he recommended, walked up Duke Street he perhaps saw a nurse maid tending a toddler. On September 25 1793, in a house a few doors down from the Union Newsroom, a daughter was born to Mr George Browne and his wife Felicia Wagner Browne who, despite her name, was of an Italian family. The baby was baptised with the name of her mother. As she grew up she proved precocious, always fascinated by books and constantly amazing her parents by her ability to read and write. If they delighted in their daughter, the Brownes had many other troubles. The Napoleonic Wars had done much to restrict Liverpool's trade and the father's business suffered as a result. Poverty led the family to leave Liverpool in 1800 and settle in North Wales, first at Gwrych and later at St Asaph. Browne emigrated to Canada in the hope of a new fortune but it was never attained and he died there in 1812, the same year in which the young Felicia married an indigent army officer, Captain Hemans.

---

* The dock may be passed round, at the pleasure and convenience of the party.
† *St Thomas's Church*, being so near at hand, may readily be viewed, by stepping aside to the right, opposite the *obelisk*.

House in Duke Street. Drawing by James Brierley

This magnificent mansion indicates how Duke Street was the first area to be devloped as a residential suburb by the wealthy mercantile elite. The house shown here was built in 1768 by Richard Kent, a merchant. Subsequently it became the home of Moses Benson. Benson is another example of the successful man who from humble beginnings was able to make a fortune in the developing Liverpool trade. He was born in Lancashire in 1738 and made a fortune in the West Indies before returning to Liverpool and to an estate he purchased in Shropshire. He became a Justice of the Peace and a public benefactor, paying for the building of St James' Free School which he endowed with £1,000. Benson died in 1806 and was buried at St James' Church.

Photo: Len Fender

Felicia was already an established author. At the age of 15, in 1808, her poems dedicated to the Prince of Wales were published. Under the patronage of William Roscoe (see page 140) her literary career flourished. Her output included poems, novels and plays. In the first half of the nineteenth century Felicia Hemans was one of the most widely read and popular literary figures – something of a national heroine. After her death in 1835 her reputation declined. Today, only one of her poems has achieved any sort of immortality and that largely in the field of parody. 'Casabianca' records the bravery and devotion of the son of

Admiral Casabianca during the battle of the Nile (1 August 1798). People who have never heard of Mrs Hemans know how 'The boy stood on the burning deck'.

The other near contemporary resident of Duke Street was a hero to some but a villain to others. John Bellingham was not a native of Liverpool but was born at St Neots in Huntingdonshire, the son of a land surveyor and a gentleman's daughter. Their family life in St Neots broke down when the father showed signs of incipient madness. The Bellinghams moved to London and John was apprenticed to a jeweller from whom he ran away. A relative, Mr Daw, acquired a commission for John in the service of the East India Company and paid to equip him with his uniforms and camp furniture. Bellingham sailed for India but the ship was wrecked and he returned to London, all ideas of a military career forgotten. Again, Mr Daw acted as his patron but John lost his money as a result of a fire and became a bankrupt in March 1794. Shortly afterwards, he obtained employment with a firm of merchants trading with Archangel in Russia. He became liable for a substantial debt in Russia and was arrested there. He blamed the British government for their failure to assist him but investigation by the consul showed his detention was perfectly legitimate. On his release and return he visited Ireland, where he married Mary Anne Neville before moving to Liverpool (1804). There he took a house on the north side of Duke Street, near Slater Street. He set up in business as an insurance broker while his wife traded as a milliner.

He persistently petitioned the government over what he saw as the injustice of the actions of the Russian authorities but was told no interference was possible. His mental condition became increasingly unstable and he manifested violent rages against the government. On Monday, 11 May 1812 he spent the day in London, with a lady friend. At about five o'clock he left her and went to the Palace of Westminster. He had bought a pair of pistols for four guineas (£4.20) and was wearing a special coat with a deep pocket to contain them. On arrival at Parliament he loitered near the door of the lobby. When the Prime Minster, Spencer Perceval, entered Bellingham shot him at point blank range and Perceval died instantly. Bellingham was seized and after a trial on 15 May was condemned to death and executed on 17 May. Spencer Perceval was one of the least distinguished of British Prime Ministers but for the melancholy distinction of being the only one assassinated.

The View of the Mount, *c.* 1790

This terrace, adjacent to the former quarry on the ridge above the town, had been developed in 1779 as a place of fashionable amusement. It provided a pleasant, rural promenade with magnificent views over the river and the town of Liverpool, as will be appreciated by any visitor to the Anglican Cathedral today. Some visitors came in search of the mineral spring which had been discovered in the rock wall of the quarry and which was reputed to be beneficial in the treatment of eye infections.

The first turning on the left hand, after entering *Pitt-street*, leads into *Duke-street*. In this avenue, called *York-street*, is an iron foundry belonging to the Coalbrookdale company.

The view up Duke-street, has always a pleasing effect, even to an inhabitant who sees it daily. For, notwithstanding a want of exact uniformity, as the street is more than half a mile long, has a gradual acclivity, increases in width as it ascends, is always clean, and the houses all neat, many elegant; with scarce an interruption of a shop, public house or warehouse; the effect must necessarily be engaging.

The bend in the street relieves the eye from the confusion that would ensue from too many objects in so extended a view, and leaves the imagination something to expect; and in which it will be disappointed by what succeeds.

In looking down when about the middle part of the street, the tops of the masts of ships, in the dock already passed, may be seen.

Near the top of the street, on the right hand, is an intended street, called *Great George-street*; which promises to form a good street. From hence the spire of St. George's church may be viewed to advantage.*

At the top of the street, on the left, branches off *Rodney-street*; so called, after the gallant admiral of that name; and will make a very handsome street.

Duke-street was the first attempt at embellished extension the town experienced; and was considered an airy retreat from the more busy and confined parts of the town. As it was begun without a regular design, its architecture is variable. Yet from its favoured access, elevation and other natural advantages, it must, especially the upper parts, when completed in the improving style of building, preserve that decided superiority over every other part of the town it originally possessed.

At the top of Duke-street will be observed, the opening of a subterraneous passage, that leads to a *delf*, or *quarry*, from whence stone is procured for the construction of the docks and public edifices. The stones are cut out of the solid rock, in such shapes and sizes as the purposes they are adapted to require.

An inclination to the right, leads to the *Mount*, or *St. James's Walk*; where we enter (on foot†) upon a gravelled terrace, 400 yards long. It has been compared to the terrace at Windsor. From hence we have a very extensive prospect, across the *Mersey*, of the north part of Cheshire, in front; and the distant mountains of

---

* Most of the public edifices may be viewed thus advantageously from different parts of the skirts of the town.

† A *horse-block* is placed near the entrance of the walk.

The Stone Delph, 1772, sketch by Matthew Gregson

The ridge of New Red Sandstone which underlies Liverpool provided a rich source of the building stone which was in widespread demand for the new developments of the town At this period, two quarries or, as they were known in the Lancashire dialect, delphs, were being worked. One was located on Brownlow Hill on the site now occupied by the Victoria Building of the University of Liverpool. The other and larger quarry, depicted here, was on St James' Mount, and later became a cemetery which is now overlooked by the Anglican Cathedral. Two windmills stood at either end of the delph while the western rim provided a promenade.

Flintshire and Denbighshire in North Wales, which fill up the back ground. The view of the interior, eastward, is very limited. From an elevated part of the *walk*, in a north-east direction, the village of *Edge-hill* has a good effect.

On facing the river, in a south-west direction, on the left, at about the distance of twenty miles, lies *Chester*, which may be discerned in clear weather.

A little to the right of the direction of Chester, and nearly over a spire steeple in Cheshire, at eleven miles distance, is *Park Gate*, on the east bank of the *Dee*. In a yet more straight direction, a little to the right of a prominent windmill in Cheshire, appears a beautifully indented, smooth chasm in the Denbighshire mountains, which forms a valley that leads to Llewnny bleach works, on the eastern confine of the delightful Vale of Clwyd. Cambden fancied these mountains to resemble fortifications. The breaks are not so irregular as in most mountainous situations; yet it requires a fanciful imagination, to admit the similitude.

These beautiful passes, mountains and vales, now so happy, retired and peaceful as to constitute a true *arcadia*, were formerly scenes of blood, during the contests of the natives with their different invaders; so that in finally losing what they esteemed to valuable, their independence as a distinct nation, they have obtained a share of protection, quiet and comfort, that can in no part of the world be exceeded. The difficult access and language of

The Rock Perch

The rocky outcrops on the northeast point of the Wirral Peninsula were such a great danger to ships entering the Mersey that they were the site of the first navigational aids provided for the port of Liverpool. A 'Perch' or wooden beacon was erected to mark the Black Rock in 1683 and remained in place until its accidental demolition by a ship in 1821. The substantial beacon was topped by a wind vane as an additional aid to the ships. The landscape of the North Wales coast depicted in this drawing is highly imaginative.

the country, while they exclude, in a great degree, the refinements
of society from the inhabitants, prevent the introduction of many
of its vices and follies, and still preserve them in quiet possession
of their native simplicity of habits and manners.

In passing still more to the right, or northward, the eye loses
the more distant Welch mountains, and becomes engaged with the
nearer Cheshire hills; especially that of *Bidston*; on which may be
perceived, to the right of a windmill, the *light-house* and *signal poles*.

Immediately on the right of the light-house, the break in the
hill affords a beautiful prospect of the sea, whereby ships may be
seen at a great distance, in the direction in which they come from
and go to sea. On that low part of the land, may be seen another
light-house; and nearly immediately behind the first, is the Hotel
at High-lake, distant about ten miles.

The eye being extended yet farther to the right, reaches the
most northern extremity of the Cheshire shore (a narrow point,
called the *Rock*, round which every vessel passes in coming in
and going out of the harbour) and then becomes lost in the vast
expanse of the Irish Sea.

The opposite shore of the *Mersey*, with the ferry-houses on its
bank; the river, with the vessels sailing and riding at anchor*; and
the town, skirted along its margin with the masts of ships in the
docks, with its towers and spires; all so immediately under the
eye; has a good effect.

The interest of this engaging prospect will be considerably
varied, not only by the weather, but by the direction of the wind.
The easterly winds, from blowing the smoke of the town over the
river, obscure the view; while the westerly winds, in clear weather,
particularly favour it.

The grove and shrubbery, behind the terrace, may be entered by
a wicket on the on the right of the avenue leading to the building,
every day except Sunday. The building was formerly a tavern, but
now converted into different private dwellings. The terrace and

---

* Ships frequently lie at anchor under the Cheshire shore, waiting for a fair wind
to go to sea.

grove are both made ground; the soil and materials having been carried thither for the purpose. The greatest part of the grove has been filled up, from the depth of the adjoining quarry, after removing the stone.

As the *walk* and adjoining grounds belong to the *corporation*, they have determined to prevent any buildings being erected in front, that may interrupt the prospect towards the river; it is obvious, therefore, that if a certain space, in front, was converted into pleasure ground, it would have a charming effect; and would be done at little expence, compared with that behind the walk.

Before we quit this engaging spot, let it be observed, that its beauties have long ago been sung by a *native bard**, under the title of '*Mount Pleasant, a Poem*'.

On leaving the walk, at the extremity opposite to where we entered it, we take a direction towards the river, down the road which passes by *St. James's Church*. The road which we then cross, leads, on the left, to *Toxteth park*, or *High park*; the first on the right, is Great George-street, already passed at the opposite end; and the second, *St. James's-street*, so called from leading to the church of that name. Here a good perspective of the beautiful spire of St. Thomas's is procured; although a lofty warehouse obscures the lower or tower part. This street will be perceived to terminate with a church at each end.

Continuing in a straight direction to the river down *Parliament-street* (a most unappropriate name) we have directly before us, over the river, a white house; which is *Birkenhead Priory*; with the remains of an Abbey, whose ivy-clad ruins yet remain to characterize it. The chapel is perfect, and now used as a place of worship. One or two hanging villages on the opposite shore are discovered from hence.

At the bottom of this street or road (which limits the boundary of Liverpool, all on the left being held under the Earl of *Sefton*, and named *Harrington*) on the left, is a road which leads to a *mill*, at a half a mile distance, that is worked by the *tide*; which, no

---

* Author of *Lorenzo de Medici*.

doubt, is a singularitly, as a patent was obtained for it. A lofty irregular building on the right, is the *Oil-house*; for the purpose of preparing the oil from the blubber of the whale, annually brought from *Greenland*; the smell from which is so offensive, during the process, as to be very disagreeable, even at some distance in the direction of the wind, although no way hurtful. It will be advisable to pass it on the windward side, to avoid the smell.

Having passed the Oil-house (fortunate, if without offence to the olfactory nerves) we break in upon the

QUEEN'S DOCK.

The newest, largest and best finished dock in the town; being 270 yards long, and 130 broad; comprising an area of 35,100 square yards; and finished at the expence of about 25,000l.

Crossing the end of the dock, to the left, we turn along its west side. On the right, are the ships in the dock, equipping, loading and unloading, with the greatest ease, safety and convenience; whilst on the left, are other ships, repairing in the *Graving Docks*. In these latter highly finished docks, the ships will be found as commodiously placed for repairing or altering, as when first building upon the stocks. The ship if floated hither by the tide at high water, and left dry at low water; the flood-gates are then shut, and the water afterwards excluded till the repairs are completed; when, the flood-gates being opened at low water, the dock is filled the next tide, and the ship then floated out.

Liverpool's Dock Development II

Sir Thomas Johnson, a tobacco merchant and Member of Parliament, was one of the new commercial elite of Liverpool who was to have great influence on the town as it emerged from obscurity. In 1708 Johnson approached George Sorocold, an engineer, possibly with some dock building experience, about building a wet dock at Liverpool. Sorocold expressed willingness to undertake the venture and in November 1708 the Corporation requested Johnson and Richard Norris, the town's other parliamentary representative, to seek parliamentary approval for the plan.

A wet, or water filled dock, in which ships could ride at the same level at any stage of the tide was a new concept. Earlier docks had been built, but only as places where ships could be laid up or fitted out. The plan to build a facility where cargo could be handled and ships safely moored for this purpose was revolutionary. Scorold intended a scheme by which the Pool would be isolated from the river by water-tight lock gates and the area behind the gates would be dredged and canalised. However, he died before his plan could be put into effect. He was replaced by Thomas Steers (c. 1670–1750), a former soldier, who was embarking upon a new career. The plan he propounded was bolder and more innovative than its predecessor.

View of Liverpool.

This view drawn from the location of Woodside is remarkable in the way in which it shows the buildings of the town completely dominated by the forest of masts of ships lying in the docks, which gives a graphic indication of the extent of Liverpool's trade. The Duke of Clarence, to whom the picture is dedicated was the son of George III, who after a naval career in which he caused disciplinary problems by his oppressive behaviour, became King William IV (1830–37) and was the origin of the expression 'Silly Billy'.

Steers proposed that the stream, which fed the Pool, should be culverted and that a stone tank should be constructed in the mouth of the estuary, with lock gates at its seaward end and joined to the Mersey by a short entrance passage. On this channel a half-tide basin with a graving dock for ship repairs was to be built. A wooden pier projected into the river which allowed ships entering the basin or leaving the dock to moor whilst waiting for favourable conditions. The area of land not enclosed within the dock would be filled in and on the reclaimed land the Corporation would erect warehouses and other buildings. The rents from these warehouses would help to defray the building costs of the dock.

By 1710 the scheme was ready for presentation to Parliament in order to obtain an authorising Act. The matter was explained thus. '... so difficult and dangerous, [was entrance to the port] that great numbers of strangers and others have frequently lost their lives, with ships and goods, for want of proper landing, buoys, and other directions into it; and more especially for want of a convenient wet dock or basin'. An additional charge was placed on all shipping in the Mersey to pay the costs of construction. This proposal aroused organised opposition from the cheese merchants of Cheshire, whose coasters would now have to pay dues towards the cost of a dock they would never use. Their protests were overruled and the Corporation authorised to raise £6,000, a totally inadequate sum for the project. Steers was appointed Dock Engineer in 1710 and work began. The dock was roughly rectangular and enclosed three and a half acres. It was lined with stone and brick, some of which came from the demolition of the castle, the remainder being quarried locally.

By 31 August 1715 the dock, if not fully completed, was opened for use. The local diarist Nicholas Blundell was there 'I went to Leverpoole and saw the *Mulberry, the Batchelor* & the *Robert* all in the Dock, they came in this morning & were the first ships as ever went into it; the *Mulberry* was first ... at the lower end of Red Cross street I saw an ox roasting'.

The new dock was a great success. Plans were drawn up for the building of additional docks, utilising what had been learned by the pioneering experience of what was soon known as 'The Old Dock'. The pattern was set and the new docks were built on reclaimed land between the river and the rising ground of the shore line. With the opening of the first wet dock Liverpool was launched on the path that was to be the foundation of its greatness as a city and port.

Foot passage over the gates of the two graving docks, afford an opportunity of going upon the *pier*; from the wall of which, a very extended view, up and down the river, may be obtained; as also a pleasing landscape of the opposite shore. A new oil-house is building there.

The flood-gates of the Queen's Dock are, as will be observed, of the same construction with those of the graving docks; only, that being designed to retain the water *in* the dock, they are hung in a contrary direction. – A pleasing cascade may often be observed from these gates at low water. – The drawbridge is a finished piece of workmanship, and does great credit to the artist, Mr MORRIS. The gates are 25 feet high, and 42 feet wide.

On looking from the bridge toward the river, we see the *entrance* from the river into the *bason* before us; which latter becomes dry at low water, and hence is called a *dry dock*. This entrance and bason serve also the purposes of the adjoining *King's Dock*. This narrow entrance and bason are highly essential; for in stormy weather, the swell of the sea would endanger the flood-gates, if they were exposed to the open river; and in the same weather, the ships could not be got safely into the dock, if opportunity was not given to check their velocity before they reached the gates; which, in the sea phrase, is *bringing up*; and which could not be done if they were left to be acted upon by the wind and waves, and the current of the tides, the powers of which are chiefly broken off by the *piers* which form the narrow entrance; where ropes from the ship can be made fast, to check its speed. Several ships can come into this outer dock, as into an antichamber, in quick succession, and there remain in safety, to be conducted through the opened gates of the interior dock, at the leisure of the parties concerned. The same advantages also accrue in going out of the dock into the river. A *buoy* is placed in the centre of the dry dock, to fix ropes to, for the purpose of assisting in the docking and undocking of the ships.

HOMER'S description of the port of Ithaca, on the landing of Ulysses, is here exemplified:

> 'Two craggy rocks projecting to the main,
> The roaring winds tempestuous rage restrain;
> Within, the waves in softer murmurs glide,
> And ships secure without their halsers ride.'
>   ODYS – BOOK XIII

Also in the harbour of the Lestrigons, the allusions, excepting the latter part of the second line, are not less striking:

> 'Within a long recess a bay there lies,
> Edg'd round with cliffs, high pointing to the skies;
> The jutting shores that swell on either side,
> Contract its mouth and break the rushing tide.
> Our eager sailors seize the fair retreat,
> And bound within the port their crouded fleet;
> For here retired the sinking billows sleep,
> And smiling calmness silvers o'er the deep.'
>   ODYS – BOOK X

What the poet's imagination feigned, is here chiefly realized by art.

The walls and constructions of and about the docks, are of stone, dug out of the quarry above; and all the ground about us is artificial, being an incroachment upon the river, and filled up with earth and other materials brought from the quarry and higher ground.

The salary of the *Dock-master* is 105l. a year; whose office is to regulate the internal decorum of the dock, by allotting the positions of the ships in their loading and unloading; to direct the management of the flood-gates; and to attend to the docking and undocking of the ships at the times of the tide when the gates are open so that the ships can come in and go out; for without such a *regulator*, who is obliged to act with impartiality, according to existing circumstances, confusion and consequent injury would regularly ensue. This dock, at present, is chiefly occupied by American ships, those from the Greenland fishery, and others under repair. Passing on, we immediately come to the

KING'S DOCK;

Made a few years before the Queen's; not so large as the Queen's; being 290 yards long, and 90 wide; comprising an area of 26,100 square yards; and finished at an expence of about 20,000l. The gates are 25 feet high, and 42 feet wide. A very commodious swivel foot-bridge, gives a passage over the gut to the pier, when the dock gates open.

Continuing along the east side of the King's Dock, we approach a long, low building, on the right; which is the TOBACCO WAREHOUSE; for the lodgment of all the tobacco imported. It was erected by the Corporation of Liverpool, and is rented at the annual sum of 500l. by Government, for the purpose of storing or lodging all the *tobacco* imported here, until the duties are paid. For this purpose, the extent of quay opposite this warehouse, is the only place in the port where tobacco can be landed. By this means, the tobacco is immediately rolled into the warehouse on landing; is there examined, weighed and secured; and thus preserved from that smuggling and pilfering so much complained of in the London river; and to prevent which, the necessity of *wet docks* there, has been so strenuously urged. When the manufacturer wants a hogshead, or more, of his tobacco, he sends the duty, and the tobacco is delivered accordingly.

This may, of the kind, be deemed an elegant building. It is 210 feet long, and 180 broad; and will contain 7000 hogsheads.

The *King's Dock* is frequented by ships from America, for the purpose of unloading their several products. Also by our own and those of the northern states from the Baltic, &c. with timber and naval stores; the spacious contiguous yards and warehouses being well adapted to their reception.

The *salary* of the Dock-master is 105l. a year. – A singularity attended the opening of this dock. One of the three ships that are recorded in history to have carried troops from hence to Ireland, to raise the siege of Londonderry, in 1688, entered this dock on the first day of its being opened in 1788; just 100 years afterward. The coincidence of circumstances is not less surprising than the extraordinary *age* of the vessel, a brig, which still continues to trade between Ireland and Liverpool, and is called the *Port-a-Ferry*.

Liverpool and Inland Waterways I

The success of any port depends on the extent of its hinterland and the ease of communications throughout that region. Consequently, throughout the late seventeenth and the whole of eighteenth centuries, the improvement of Liverpool's lines of communication was of paramount importance. While road transport remained difficult and expensive – though it should be noted that Lancashire's first turnpike road (1720) linked the port to Prescot and was utilised for the carriage of coal and pottery – waterbourne traffic was the most attractive option.

Initially, attention concentrated on the improvement of existing rivers to make them more suitable for navigation. In Lancashire attention focused on linking Liverpool to Manchester and to the other industrial centres of production. River navigations enjoyed a vogue in Restoration England and half-hearted proposals were made in the 1660s and 1670s for the improvement of the Mersey and the Weaver, but no work was put in hand. In 1691 Thomas Pattern, a Warrington merchant, had obtained an Act to improve the Mersey for vessels as far as his wharf. He wrote of the impediment provided by the salmon traps and goes on 'What vast advantage would it be to Liverpool if the river was made navigable to Manchester and Stockport ... since I made it navigable to Warrington ... there have been sent to and from Liverpool 2000 tons of goods per year'. Patten's dream was accomplished in 1721 when, under the auspices of Thomas Steers, approval was given for the development of the Mersey navigation to Manchester, which opened in 1734.

In 1712 Steers was employed to prepare a plan to make the river Douglas navigable between Wigan and Tarleton, on the estuary of the Ribble. It was seen as an artery by which coal could be shipped to Liverpool, as well as to the whole north Lancashire coast. It was not until 1720 that the bill was approved in Parliament but it suffered in the crash that followed the collapse of the South Sea Company; the plan took a further twenty years to reach completion but proved useful and significant.

Perhaps the most important navigation for Liverpool was that of the River Weaver. After attempts to obtain Parliamentary approval in 1711, 1715, 1718 and 1720 the Bill was granted in 1721. Penetrating deep into the Cheshire salt field, the navigation led to the development of the recently discovered Marbury rock salt mines, which challenged the traditional methods of extracting brine from the subterranean lakes or wichs This navigation also opened up a route for agricultural produce, and facilitated the transportation of manufactured goods, iron, pottery and coal from the west Midlands and Staffordshire.

The last navigation that was to improve the development of Liverpool's communications was the proposal to make the Sankey Brook, which ran from the St Helens area to the Mersey at Widnes, navigable. The impetus for this venture came from the colliery owners of St Helens, who were finding that the coal transported down the navigations could be sold more cheaply in Liverpool than their product which had to be carried by road. On 25 October 1755 with the support of the Corporation, they petitioned Parliament 'for making the river or brook called Sankey Brook and three branches thereof navigable'. The bill was approved and hidden amongst the small print was permission to make 'cuts', i.e. to make artificial channels to shorten bends or avoid shallow places. It was soon realised by Henry Berry, the engineer and by John Ashton, the treasurer and executive member of the board, that the brook was too small and insignificant to be used for boats. The two men formed a covert design to utilise the permissive clause to make 'cuts' to their advantage and constructed, for almost the full length of the Brook, an artificial channel. The Sankey navigation opened in November 1757 and proved highly successful. It was, in effect, Britain's first canal.

Liverpool and Inland Waterways II

Eagerly watching the completion of the Sankey Brook Canal was a
wealthy land owner in the North West, the Duke of Bridgewater,
whose concern was the carriage of coal between his mines at Worsley
and the markets in Manchester. He realised that the construction of a
seven mile canal between these two points would solve his difficulties.
The engineers were James Brindley, a Staffordshire millwright and John
Gilbert, Bridgewater's estate manager. The line included some complex
engineering to build an aqueduct over the Mersey and Irwell navigation
at Barton. When the canal opened in July 1761 the price of coal in
Manchester was halved.

Bridgewater was inspired to extend the canal along the southern
bank of the Mersey to Runcorn where it descended a flight of locks to
enter the river. Despite delays in completion, due to the intransigence
of the Brooke family at Norton Priory, by 1772 the whole line was
complete and proved popular and economical. It formed a vital link
between the two urban centres of Lancashire. At Liverpool the Duke
built a dock where his 'Flats' – a fleet of forty two each of 50 tons
– could load and discharge their cargo.

No sooner was that canal finished than Bridgewater, in partnership
with Josiah Wedgwood, embarked on a project to construct a canal to
link the rivers Trent and Mersey. The first enabling Act of Parliament
was in 1766 but the difficulties of engineering ensured that it was
not until May 1777 that the canal was in operation. It was to be the
first link in a national canal system which linked the Mersey region
to the industrial Midlands, and, eventually to London. In 1796 The
Corporation of Liverpool supported the extension of the canal which
had been 'productive of very important advantages to Liverpool by
opening extensive commercial intercourse with many populous towns
and large manufactories in the interior part of the kingdom'.

The completion of the Leeds Liverpool canal between 1770 and
1816 involved a great deal of spectacular engineering work before
the link between Liverpool and the navigable river Aire at Leeds was
established. Though originally projected as a cross country route
from the Irish Sea to the North Sea, this proved much less important
than the traffic on the western portion of the very circuitous route
from Liverpool via Wigan, Blackburn and Burnley. A great deal of the

expansion of the cotton industry in Lancashire can be ascribed to the opportunity for mills to be able to import their raw materials and fuel from the port of Liverpool by canal and to dispatch their finished products on the return journey. Thus Lancashire cottons could be sent easily and cheaply through Liverpool to a worldwide market.

It is usual to see the railways as providing the vital links on which the Industrial Revolution was based, but this is a misconception. For the first fifty years of industrialisation it was the inland waterways which provided the arteries of trade. Early canal companies made high profits in their first few years, often over 50%. Goods of all sorts, but especially those which were heavy or bulky such as cotton, wool, coal, iron, timber, bricks, salt and grain filled hundreds of boats. In the 1820s it is calculated that 1 in 27 of the national working population was employed in the canal industry. The grooves worn by tow ropes in the old stonework of a canal bridge, or in the iron bollards at a lock, are an indicator of the intensity of the traffic. As Dr Moss tells us, there were canal express passenger services as well. Boat travel was often smoother and quicker than by road. However, canal travel was expensive – in 1821 the first class fare for the nine hour journey from Liverpool to Wigan was 3s. 6d.

The original Liverpool terminus of the Leeds and Liverpool canal was at Leeds Street where some buildings can still be seen. In the 1850s a branch from Vauxhall to the new Stanley Dock gave the canal boats direct access to the dock system.

———————

The interposing ground between these docks and the river, is chiefly employed for timber yards and ship building.

Turning the corner of the tobacco warehouse, we obtain a view of its other fronts. The street into which we enter is called *Wapping*, aptly enough named after the same in London. The large warehouses which here present themselves, are chiefly for the storing of corn. In this neighbourhood we shall find *roperies, anchor-smithies, block-makers, sail-makers*, and every business connected with the *naval department*, in great abundance; together with a number of *public houses*, for the cooking and accommodation of the shipping; for as fires and candles are not suffered on board the ships in the docks, for obvious reasons, public houses become more necessary.

Directing our course northward, we soon reach a small dock, which belongs to the *Duke of Bridgewater*, for the use of his flats (forty-two in number, of fifty tons each) that convey goods by the communication of the *Runcorn canal*, sixteen miles up the river, to all the interior manufacturing towns and neighbourhoods of *Manchester*, the *Staffordshire potteries*, &c. &c.* to an amazing extent. The adjoining warehouse, is for the security of the goods before and after they are shipped and unshipped; to which purpose the adjoining yard is also applied. Proceeding a little farther, we approach the

SALT-HOUSE DOCK;

So called from former salt works on the right, where the common salt, we use, was made from the native rock. This manufactury is removed many miles higher up the river, to a place called *Garston*, to the great benefit of the town; as the vast quantity of coal smoke emitted from it, made it very offensive. – This was the second made dock. The upper end, on which we enter, is chiefly employed as a receptacle for ships that are laid up. The lower parts are mostly for corn and timber ships. The form is irregular. It comprizes an area of 21,928 square yards; and has a length of quay of 640 yards.

The space between this dock and the river, behind the building, is chiefly occupied as ship-builders yards; and some of the finest ships of their size, in the British navy, have been built there; as the *Adamant* and *Assistance* of fifty guns; and the *Phaeton, Nemesis, Success* and other fine frigates. These yards may be viewed.

Tracing the quay till we come to the flood-gates, which are 23

---

* One hundred and ten vessels of this description are employed upon the river, chiefly in conveying salt down from Northwich, &c. as also a good many others, in bringing down coals from the Sankey canal.

feet high, and 34 feet wide; and which, with the draw-bridge, are inferior in point of construction to those at the Queen's Dock; we open upon a very large *bason*; which is dry at low water, and hence called a *dry dock*, as we observed at the Queen's Dock. Keeping to the right, we presently reach the

OLD DOCK;

The first dock we met with on the outset of our ramble. From the *draw-bridge*, we see, towards the river, the gut or entrance into the bason from the river; and that the gut and bason accommodate both this and the Salt-house Dock. Looking up the dock, we observe the Custom House, we before passed, facing us at the other end. This first constructed dock has been made about 75 years. Its walls were originally of brick. It is 200 yards long; of irregular breadth, but which may average 80 yards; with an area of 16,832 square yards. The gates are 23 feet high, and 34 feet wide.

This dock is a receptacle of West India and African ships, as it is contiguous to the warehouses of the merchants concerned in those branches of commerce. Also Irish traders, and vessels from Portugal, Spain, and the Mediterranean. The surrounding houses are altogether public houses, or shops with such articles of wearing apparel, &c. as are most commonly wanted by seamen. Adjoining the outside of the gates of this dock, is a *slip*, where fish is most commonly landed from the different fishing boats from Ireland, Scotland, and the more adjacent neighbouring coasts.

As we proceed along the *dry dock*, we observe a great many small vessels, chiefly sloops with one mast each, and which are coasting traders, mostly from the northern coast, extending to Scotland; as may be observed by painted boards, hung upon the most conspicuous parts of the rigging, denoting the places they are bound to. This trade is very extensive, consisting of the importation of corn and other provisions, slates and the different natural productions of the country; and of the exportation coastways of every article of our West India produce, the Mediterranean, Portugal, Spanish and Baltic trade. This is generally a busy, crowded place. Coasting along this dry dock, we at length arrive at the south gates and drawbridges of St. George's Dock.

Dock Development III

From the opening of the Dock in 1715, Liverpool's trade expanded rapidly and the original construction proved inadequate. By 1737 it was decided that a new wet dock, together with various other improvements to the port facilities, should be made and a further Act of Parliament was obtained. The new dock, which was designed by Thomas Steers, – now a power in the life of Liverpool – was to open off the entrance channel to the old dock. Originally known as South Dock, it was, later, to be named Salthouse Dock, after the refinery operated by John Blackburne, which was located in the area. Construction began in 1738 but was slow, partly because of the nature of the ground and also because of the lack of funds available. It was not until 1758 that the dock opened to shipping. The area had been the site of several ship-building yards and this activity continued in the vicinity, building both merchant and warships.

By the time the new dock was in service, work had begun on yet another dock project. Steers died in 1750 and the post of Engineer was taken on by Steers' former assistant, Henry Berry (1719–1812). It was Berry who designed and supervised the construction of George's Dock which extended north from the former graving or dry dock at the entrance to Salthouse Dock and was also accessed from a new basin at its northern end. As a result, the dock ran on a north-south axis. In 1793, a large block of warehouses was erected between the dock and the Strand. Designed by John Hope, they comprised seventeen warehouses, some as much as thirteen stories high. The block was destroyed in a huge fire in 1802 to be replaced by another, more sophisticated design by John Foster. Despite local legend, these warehouses, named the Goree after an African slaving port, had no connection with that trade. George's Dock was abandoned for commercial use and filled in 1900. The famous group of buildings comprising The Royal Liver Buildings, the Cunard Offices and the Port of Liverpool Building were constructed on the site.

Returning the way we came, we reach the south end of *St. George's Dock*; but instead of passing in a direction along its quay, we keep on towards the river. A circumstance occurred on this spot, which cannot be passed over. – the docility of the *cart-horses* of Liverpool, perhaps exceeds that of any in the kingdom, or even the world. The carters usually direct their horses motions by word only, without touching the reins; and can make them go to the right or the left, backward or forward by the word of command, with as much precision as a company of soldiers. A *parrot*, of no mean parts; as it appears; by frequent hanging out from one of these houses facing the dock, had acquired a variety of language; and more especially that particular part which so frequently requires the horse to back his load, to discharge it into the ship in the dock. A carter having unfortunately left his cart with the back to the dock, *pol*, in a garrulous mood, unluckily happened to cry, *back – back – back* – several times so distinctly and loudly, that the well-tutored animal, obeying the word of command, actually backed the cart, so as to precipitate it and himself into the dock. The horse was preserved.

That two brute animals, of totally different species, perfect strangers to each other, should be capable, without any assistance, of directing and executing a regular action by means of the human language; is a curiosity perhaps unparalleled in the history of the world.

On the left, as we advance, lies the *Manchester old quay*, the resort of that company's *flats*, 32 in number, which convey goods to and from Manchester daily, all the way by the river, without entering a canal, as is done by those of the Duke of Bridgewater.

We now arrive at the *river*, and have, on the right, a *terrace* 230 yards long, which is purposely designed for a *public walk*, as carriages are not suffered to come upon it, and is called the *Parade*.

The view from hence can perhaps be no where excelled, especially at or a little before high water, and particularly at spring tides; when a number of vessels, of all descriptions, moving in all directions, so near at hand, forms a moving picture, highly engaging and interesting; and which, from the variety it always

A View of BUILDINGS. Nova Scotia, 1830.

Nova Scotia
Drawing by James Brierley

The name of this area seems to have been derived from its isolated location on the quay of George's Dock. In this way it was similar to the adjacent area of Mann Island. The terrace contained both housing and establishments intended to satisfy the various requirements of the ships and sailors.

affords, is entertaining even to those who see it most frequently. At all times, the view up and down the river is fine. At the other end of the Parade, is a *pier* that projects father into the river, from whence a more extended prospect can be obtained.

The houses on the opposite shore, are the *ferry-houses* before mentioned. Down the river, we observe the *rock point*, with a *guide post* upon its extremity; round which the ships pass and repass to and from sea. A little on this side the *rock*, may be seen the *powder magazines*; where all the gunpowder for the use of the ships, and other purposes, is kept. They are placed at that distance (about three miles) to prevent bad consequences to the town in case of accident; they are also much out of the way of accident from fire. Ships often lie off there at anchor, sheltered from the westerly winds, under the high land, waiting for a fair wind to proceed to sea. Many years ago, a ship, at anchor there, blew up.

The concussion was considerable in the town. Ships in the docks are not permitted to have gunpowder on board.

A little down the river on this side, will be observed the *Fort*; and, at a great distance farther down, two lofty *pillars*, which are the *Formby land-marks*.

On the left of this *pier*, is a *sloping road* or *slip*, which gradually descends to *low water mark*, where a number of *boats* are constantly lying for the purpose of being hired to convey passengers, horses, &c. to the different *ferrys* on the opposite shore; as also

Fort and Lighthouse

The rocky outcrops which marked the entrance to the Mersey on the Cheshire side were a dangerous hazard to shipping. After the accidental demolition of the Perch in 1821 the stone-built lighthouse was projected. A proposal to emplace guns for defence of the harbour was rejected and instead the fort of 1808 on the adjacent Red Noses was to be strengthened. In 1826 a new fort designed and built under the supervision of Captain Kitson R.E at a cost of £26,995 0s. 8d. was begun and opened on 30 April 1830. In this engraving the vessel bearing the numeral 7 on its sail is one of the pilot cutters, while the boat in the foreground gives a vivid impression of the sailing ferries and the conditions to be found on board them. The crossing could be long and arduous. In 1698 when Celia Fiennes crossed, the journey took an hour and a half, in a boat that could carry 10 people and some horses.

View of Liverpool from Seacombe, 1816

This panorama of the waterfront depicts the principal buildings and landmarks of the town. They can be identified from left to right as the dome of St Paul's church, that of the Town Hall, the new tower and lantern (only completed the previous year) of St Nicholas' Church. George's dock can be discerned behind the two ships in the river. St Thomas's church is visible and the King's and Queen's docks. In the foreground two ferries approach the landing spot where a ship is being careened to remove marine growths. On the river in the distance a steamer can be made out. This is probably the *Elizabeth*, introduced the previous year as a ferry boat. Passengers found the steam engine alarming and it was quickly replaced by a horse-operated treadmill.

for pleasure, up and down the river, as the wind and tide will permit. Although there are many conveniences for taking the water at the other docks, similar to this; yet this is much the most commodious, cleanest and safest. The others are mostly within the dry docks; so that the gut or entrance to the dock must be passed through, which is oftentimes tedious, and even unsafe, from the number of vessels generally passing in and out about high water, as the following melancholy instance will explain.

Several large *ferry-boats*, filled with passengers to Chester fair, were hauling out of the Old Dock gut along the north wall, the wind blowing fresh from south west; when suddenly a very large ship, hitherto unnoticed, was coming full upon them, from the river, with considerable velocity, and in such a manner and direction as no human efforts could avert; as the boats were too numerous to have them all got out of the way, and no time to get the passengers out of the boats upon the quay. In this terrifying situation, as the ship – with a sea monster's head, as if to aggravate the horror – approached very near the boats, the cries of distress from the passengers, who seemed but too sensible of their situation, were painful indeed. Too soon the ship, without any decrease of its speed, struck one of the boats in the middle with its stem. The boat, although a large one, being close to the wall, was instantly shivered to pieces. – The shriek of distress now ceased; as every appearance of the boat and its luckless passengers was lost, and,

> 'Like the baseless fabric of a vision,
> Left not a *wreck* behind.'

In a few moments, however, baskets, hats, fragments of the boat, and immediately after the bodies of the unfortunate people, had emerged and were floating upon the surface of the water. Every assistance being given, the people, about twenty in number, men, women and children, were all, as then understood, got out of the water, many of them unhurt. Those who were most in the bottom of the boat escaped the best, as, on the complete destruction of the boat, they sunk in the water under the ship's bottom; while those who attempted to save themselves by climbing up the wall, were some of them so severely crushed as not to survive it; which was the case with one or two active young men. – The rest of the boats escaped uninjured. – Although it is some years since the above accident happened, it made too strong an impression upon the mind of the narrator, who beheld it, to be yet effaced. *This* landing place is out of a possibility of any similar accident ever happening *here*; and therefore is, on all accounts, to be preferred. The fares of the boatmen have been named.

The right wall of this *pier*, will be found to form one side of the *gut* or *entrance* into the *bason*, or dry dock, which leads to *St. George's Dock*. The opposite side of this bason is generally occupied by Welch traders. In the river, immediately before the pier, will

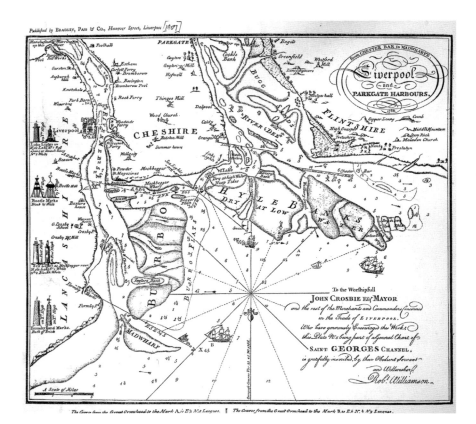

Chart of the Mersey Estuary, 1766

This chart, despite its unusual orientation, shows the approaches to both the Mersey and the Dee. The Hyle Lake is visible off the north west corner of the Wirral and the Rock channel can be traced between the Hyle, Burbo and Mockbeggar banks. The Formby and Crosby channels are shown but the complex approaches made them less used by larger ships. Depths of water are indicated by the figures along the channels. The shore and the land visible from the sea is liberally dotted with land marks. To the most important of these appropriate bearings are given and to help in recognition of marks the beacons and lighthouses are depicted on the left-hand margin.

discovered two large buoys; which are there placed for the purpose of making ropes fast to them, to assist in hauling ships out of the dock, when the wind blows into the dock. A *capstan* will be observed on the *pier*, to assist likewise in hauling ships in and out of the dock, as necessity may require. Several strong *posts*, are also placed in different situations, for similar purposes. A large *flag staff*, or *pole*, is placed here; on which, when a *flag* is *hoisted*, it denotes that the dock-gates are *open*, to receive any ships that may be coming in: when *lowered*, it apprizes those ships in the river, that the gates are *shut* so as to exclude their entrance that tide. A double *lamp* is placed upon the top of this pole, (hung upon swivels, to accommodate the raising and lowering of the pole) to direct any vessel that may have occasion to come into the dock in the dark. It is to be observed, that the same accommodations, for assisting the ships into and out of the dock, prevail at the entrances of the other docks we have passed.

'Not Buoyed or Beaconed' I

The problem of Liverpool's tidal range is discussed elsewhere (see Holden's Tide Tables p. 69) but, in the eighteenth century, the navigation of the Mersey presented many other difficulties for ships. The shape of the estuary, heavy silting and the formation of sand banks on the threshold of the river created serious and dangerous obstructions. At this time, only two channels threaded the mass of shoals and even these were liable to silting and changes of direction. The main channel, known as the Rock Channel, was best approached from the north westerly direction. Ships would round Point Lynas on Anglesey, make for the Great Ormes Head and then for Hilbre Island. At this point they entered a large, clear stretch of water off the north west corner of the Wirral peninsula, known as Hoyle or Hyle Lake. It was common practice for the ships to anchor in this natural harbour and discharge some of their cargo to reduce the draught of the vessel. Leaving Hoyle Lake, they followed the Bootle landmarks – two wooden beacons – through a narrow channel that led to the north east point of Wirral, marked by two rocky outcrops known as Black Rock and the Red Noses. These so often proved fatal to vessels that, in 1683, to mark this danger point a 'Perch', a wooden pole beacon, was erected on the Black Rock or, as it was later known, the Perch Rock. In 1821 the Perch was accidentally destroyed and the present lighthouse replaced it. The Rock Channel could also be entered via the Swash, a passage between the Burbo and Hoyle banks, thus avoiding the Hoyle Lake. The entrances to all these passages were marked by floating, wooden buoys.

The other entrance to the port, via the Formby Channel, was much less used than the Rock passage. Ships approaching from the north east passed between the Mad Wharf and Burbo Banks through a channel where only nine feet of water was to be found at low tide. They then proceeded along the coast, though the Crosby Channel and into the Mersey. There were three swatches or shallow, narrow channels through the Burbo Bank which were navigable to small ships at the highest tides.

During the eighteenth century efforts were made to facilitate the navigation of these tricky passages by the erection of navigational land marks and light houses. The earliest proposal dated from 1664, when Parliamentary approval for an Act to allow the building of privately owned lights in 'the Redd Channel', was fiercely opposed by the Liverpool Corporation. In 1719, a 101 foot brick tower was erected to serve as a leading mark for the entrance to the Formby Channel. Later, this was supplemented by a perch on the shore line. Later still, the low beacon was replaced by a brick tower. The original Formby tower was demolished in 1941 to avoid its use as a navigational mark by enemy bombers.

In 1763, the Corporation began a major programme of lighthouse building, mainly to improve the navigation of the Rock Channel, which was subjected to heavy silting. A 70-foot tower was built at Hoylake with a floating light at water level. Two further towers were built at Leasowe, only one of which remains. In 1771 these lights were supplemented by a tower built on Bidston Hill, which was rebuilt in 1872. Though the structure remains, the light was extinguished in 1913. In their early days all the lights used coal fires but these were replaced by oil lamps and the parabolic reflectors invented by William Hutchinson, the dock master of Liverpool.

Light vessels were not introduced on to the Mersey until 1813, when the *Good Intent*, a former Dutch galliot, was anchored off

View of Hilbre Island and the coast of North Wales

The artist's viewpoint is from the Hoyle Lake, looking south-west. Hilbre Island had served as the location of a mediaeval religious cell but by 1795 was the penultimate station of the semaphore system which conveyed news of the arrival of ships from Point Llynas in Anglesey to Liverpool. The observatory or lookout point on Hilbre Island is still in existence. At the last point in the line – Bidston Hill – signal flags were hung to identify the various owners and vessels.

The Bootle Landmark

Located on the ridge of high land in Linacre, this beacon was visible from the Rock Channel. It provided a leading mark for ships in the Hoyle Lake or Rock Channel which would bring them safely to the mouth

of the Mersey. The landmarks were reconstructed twice during the nineteenth century and were finally demolished on the extension of the docks into Bootle in the last decades of that century

Leasowe Light House 1776 and in recent times

The light tower at Leasowe was one of the navigational aids built in 1776 as a part of a general scheme to improve the safety of the difficult approaches to Liverpool harbour. This together with the lights at Hoylake and Bidston, the North West Lightship and the beacons at Formby and Bootle were all placed to improve the navigation of the Rock Channel, and became largely redundant as the Crosby and Formby channel approach was developed in the late nineteenth and the early twentieth centuries.

COURTESY OF THE HISTORIC SOCIETY OF LANCASHIRE AND CHESHIRE.
PHOTO: LEN FENDER

Light Vessel Good Intent

This lightship, adapted from a former Dutch galliot, a type of vessel chosen for their sound construction and good sea-keeping qualities, was located at the North Western Station at the entrance to the Rock Channel in 1813. At night three white lights were shown and during the day it flew the huge blue and white flag, with the letters NW on it, that can be seen here. Subsequently, as the channels changed the lightship was moved to the Bar.

COURTESY OF THE HISTORIC SOCIETY OF LANCASHIRE AND CHESHIRE.
PHOTO. LEN FENDER

the Hoyle sandbank. At night she displayed three white lights and during the day a huge, blue flag, bearing the letters NW in white was flown, in fogs a bell was sounded. Subsequently, similar vessels were established off Formby, Crosby and in the mouth of the Dee. In 1873 the North West light vessel was relocated at the Bar. Captain Grenville Collins' (1693) observation that the Mersey was 'neither buoyed or beaconed' was no longer true.

Buoyed and Beaconed II

As the number of ships using the Mersey increased year on year during the eighteenth century, the problems of safety on the river occupied the thoughts of the Corporation. There were obvious humanitarian concerns but the loss of ships and cargo was a drain on the prosperity of the port. The development of the docks had improved the cargo handling provision, the steady development of navigational aids made the approaches to the port more secure but there was a need for experienced pilots to take charge of ships and bring them safe to anchor. Pilots were available but these were freelance men, unregulated and unsupervised, who competed for custom and often failed in their duty. In 1764 no fewer than eighteen vessels were wrecked by faulty navigation, £18,000 worth of cargo lost and seventy five people drowned.

So it was that, two years later, the Liverpool Corporation sought an Act of Parliament to establish a regulated and licensed pilot service, controlled by a pilotage committee. This group drew up a series of rules and regulations which were later embodied in the Act. The regulations laid down the equipment, training, experience and charges which were required for a pilot's licence. The Act was approved and a body of Commissioners set up which included representatives of the trading, civic and maritime community. In addition, a mechanism was created whereby a Collector of Pilots' Dues was established and the financial irregularities which had occurred were eliminated. A scale of charges was to be levied which took account of the season, whether the vessel was foreign or British and the length of the passage under pilotage.

To ensure the competence of the pilots, regulations soon followed that laid down the qualifications for a licence. The applicant must

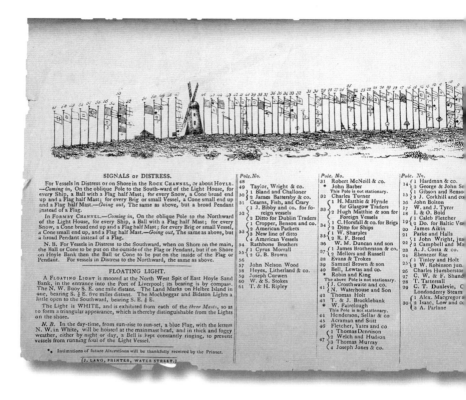

The Bidston Hill Signal Station

This particular engraving shows the signalling system at its most complicated and, though undated, dates from after the introduction of steamers. Observers in the Tower of Liverpool, or, later in its replacement office block, received the signals and passed the word through the town. The observatory from which a lookout was kept and which subsequently became both an astronomical and tidal observation point, together with the lighthouse are visible in this engraving. The sockets which held the flag poles are still to be found on Bidston Hill. The windmill shown here is still in existence and is clearly visible from the Pier Head in Liverpool.

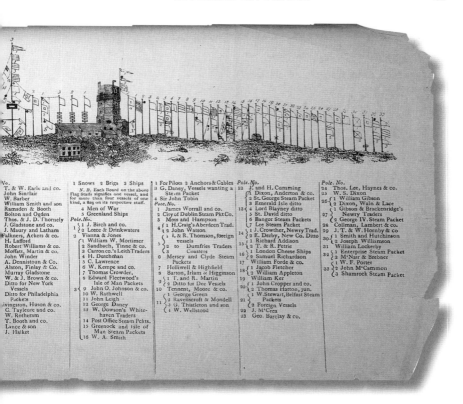

No.
T. & W. Earle and co.
John Sinclair
W. Barber
William Smith and son
Ramsden & Booth
Bolton and Ogden
Thos. & J. D. Thornely
J. Gladstone and co.
J. Maury and Latham
Falkners, Ackers & co.
H. Lafford
Robert Williams & co.
Moffatt, Martin & co.
John Winder
A. Denniston & Co.
Alston, Finlay & Co.
Murray Gladstone
W. & J. Brown & co.
Ditto for New York Vessels
Ditto for Philadelphia Packets
Livingston, Huson & co.
C. Tayleure and co.
W. Rotheram
T. Booth and co.
Lince & son
J. Halket

1 Snows 2 Brigs 3 Ships
N.B. Each Board on the above Flag Staff signifies one vessel, and for more than four vessels of one kind, a flag on its respective staff.
Pole. No.
4 Men of War
5 Greenland Ships
Pole. No.
1 { 1 J. Birch and co. / 2 Leece & Drinkwaters
2 { 1 Vianna & Jones
1 William W. Mortimer
2 Sandbach, Tinne & co.
3 Carron co.'s Leith Traders
4 H. Dutchman
5 C. Lawrence
6 W. Kempe and co.
7 Thomas Crowder.
8 Edward Fleetwood's Isle of Man Packets
3 { 9 John O. Johnson & co.
10 W. Rothwell
11 John Leigh
12 George Daney
13 W. Dowson's Whitehaven Traders
14 Post Office Steam Pckts.
15 Greenock and Isle of Man Steam Packets
16 W. A. Smith

1 For Pilots 2 Anchors & Cables
3 G. Daney, Vessels wanting a Steam Packet
4 Sir John Tobin
Pole. No.
1 James Worrall and co.
2 City of Dublin Steam Pkt Co.
3 Moss and Hampson
4 { 1 H.Craig's Aberdeen Trad. / 2 John Watson
5 { 1 J. & R. Thomson, foreign vessels / 2 to Dumfries Traders / 3 Coasters
6 Mersey and Clyde Steam Packets
7 Holliwell & Highfield
8 Barton, Irlam & Higginson
9 { 1 T. and R. Martin / 2 Ditto for Dee Vessels
10 Tennent, Moore & co.
11 { 1 George Green / 2 Ravenscroft & Mondell / 3 G. Thistleton and son / 4 W. Wellstood

Pole. No.
12 J. and H. Cumming
13 { 1 Dixon, Anderton & co. / 2 St. George Steam Packet / 3 Emerald Isle ditto / 4 Lord Blayney ditto / 5 St. David ditto / 6 Bangor Steam Packets / 7 Lee Steam Packet
14 { 1 J.Crowther, Newry Trad. / 2 E. Derby, New Co. Ditto
15 { 1 Richard Addison / 2 T. & R. Petrie
16 { 1 London Cheese Ships / 2 Samuel Richardson
17 William Forde & co.
18 { 1 Jacob Fletcher / 2 William Appleton
19 William Ker
20 { 1 John Cropper and co. / 2 Thomas Hatton, jun.
21 { 1 W.Stewart, Belfast Steam Packets / 2 Foreign Vessels
22 J. M'Crea
23 Geo. Barclay & co.

Pole. No.
24 Thos. Lee, Haynes & co.
25 W. S. Dixon
26 { 1 William Gibson / 2 Dixon, Wain & Lace
27 { 1 Gibson & Brackenridge's Newry Traders / 2 George IV. Steam Packet
28 Collman, Lambert & co.
29 J. T. & W. Hornby & co
30 { 1 Smith and Hutchinson / 2 Joseph Williamson
31 William Lockerby
32 { 1 Enterprise Steam Packet / 2 M'Nair & Brebner
33 { 1 W. F. Porter / 2 John M'Cammon / 3 Shamrock Steam Packet

be above eighteen years old, have served either three years as an apprentice in the pilot service or five years in a seagoing vessel and be competent in ship handling. He had to 'know arithmetic' and to be able to describe the harbours and waters from the Piel of Foudray to Anglesey and westward to the Isle of Man. He had to know and understand the tides and all the navigational marks. These prodigies were to go to sea in a fleet of nine cutters which were to cruise, in turn, on four stations, Angelsey, Hoylake, and Mad Wharf Buoy, while one was stationed in Liverpool to handle outward bound vessels.

Being a pilot was no sinecure. Over fifty licences were issued in 1766 and of forty one recorded names we know that sixteen were drowned when three cutters were wrecked in 1770. Life at sea was made easier for the pilots when, in 1779, a sheltered harbour with repair and replenishment facilities was established at Point Lynas on Anglesey.

In 1797, after nearly thirty years experience of the previous system, a second Pilotage Act tidied up many of the loose ends and particularly attempted to make the earnings of pilots more equitable. There were also clauses to encourage them to pay greater attention to smaller, coastal vessels.

In 1766 the original pilot's office was in Litherland's Alley off Castle Street and later in Drury Lane. In 1795 it was transferred to the tower building, which housed the gaol. It was ordered that the office should be distinguished by a large board painted with a picture of a pilot cutter and the words 'Pilot Office'. In 1819 when the tower was scheduled for demolition the office was transferred to a building in Old Church Yard adjacent to St Nicholas church. In 1861 it was moved to Princes Dock and in 1883 to a site on the dock wall at Canning Dock. This building and its adjacent boat shed is now part of the Merseyside Maritime Museum where examples of models and paintings of the pilot cutters, and later schooners, in their regulation colour scheme, can be seen The Liverpool Pilot Service after many years of diligent and sometimes heroic service was closed in the 1970s, though a service organised in a different way still exists.

From this pier and the parade, may now more distinctly be seen the *light-house* and *signal poles.** The river is here, at high water, about three quarters of a mile over; and the distance from the opposite shore to the light-house, about three miles. It is very usual, in summer and fine weather, for *parties* to cross the river, and *walk* to the light-house. The road is good, and the walk, if a trouble, is amply repaid by the charming and extensive prospect which is there displayed.† Ale, and bread and cheese, is the only fare to be met with there; except perhaps a cup of tea. Any kind of provision that may be carried thither, will be comfortably dressed and served, and every deficiency compensated by the

---

* A deliniation and explanation of the *light-house* and *signal-poles*, may be had, printed upon a card, at any of the book-sellers shops; which will afford a better description than can be given here.

† A chaise may be had at the opposite ferry-house, the *Wood-side*.

civility of the occupiers. To those who have not examined a *light-house*, it will, of course, prove a curiosity. It is lighted by a lamp of cotton wick and oil.

The idea of a bridge across the river, may possibly strike the stranger's mind. But that, if practicable, is inadmissible near the town, as it would be greatly injurious to the navigation of the river. It is however impracticable, from the depth of water and rapidity of the tides. The river is ten fathom (twenty yards) deep at low water, opposite and a considerable way above the town; and the tides frequently run at the rate of six miles an hour. It is often difficult to sail against the tide, even with a fair and strong breeze; and still more so to row a boat directly against it, as

'Scarce the boat's brawny crew the current stem,
And, slow advancing, struggle with the stream;
But if they slack their oars, or cease to strive,
Then down the stream with headlong haste they drive.

GEORGICS, BOOK I

The tide in the river rises about 30 feet at spring tides, and 21 at neap tides.

It has already been observed, that the time of high water at spring tides, is most favourable for the river *prospect* from this, the most eligible, situation on the shore. Accordingly, when high water happens any time from eleven till two o'clock, it will be proper to be here half an hour, or more, before the time of high water (which may be known by a reference to any of the Liverpool newspapers); when, a westerly wind seldom fails to bring in more or less sail. Armed ships generally salute the town with their cannon; which is answered by the bells of the adjoining church. These signals generally invite a number from the town, to behold the pleasing spectacle; and the solicitude of the relatives of those on board, frequently forms an interesting scene.

The ships of different owners have private distinct signals, which they communicate to a person always stationed at the light-house, who repeats them upon the various adjoining poles, so as to be understood here; whereby the approach of a particular ship may often be known some hours before it can be seen from the town. Would a telegraph answer a better purpose? – The ship having entered the dry dock (now filled with water) in the manner described at the Queen's dock is conducted into the inner wet dock, and there left afloat, in the most perfect security from every assailment of wind and sea.

A little before high water, the ships that are to come out of dock the present tide, are hauled* into the outer bason, then into the gut; where the sails are filled, the fastenings loosened, and, amid the usual parting salute of three cheers from the brave departing *tars*, and which is returned from the spectators on shore, the stately vessel is sent to explore her way over the dreary bosom of the vast trackless ocean, under the well founded hope of giving wealth to the individual, and of adding honour and prosperity to the British Empire.

> 'Spectators, while the ship departs the land,
> On shore with admiration gazing stand.
> BRITANNIA, riding awful on the prow,
> Surveys the vassal wave that rolls below:
> Where'er she moves, the vassal waves are seen
> To yield obsequious and confess their queen.
> Such is the sculptur'd prow – from van to rear
> Th' artillery frowns, a black tremendous tier.
> High o'er the poop, the flattering winds display,
> Th' imperial flag that rules the wat'ry sway.
> Then tow'r the masts; the canvass swells on high
> And waving streamers flutter in the sky.

---

* The frequent repetition of the nautical term, *haul*, cannot well be avoided, as none of the synonima, of draw, pull, drag, &c. are sufficiently expressive, or proper.

'With winning postures, now the wanton sails
Spread all their snares to charm th' inconstant gales:
While all to court the wand'ring breeze are plac'd,
With yards now thwarting, now obliquely brac'd.
Majestically slow, before the breeze,
In silent pomp she marches on the seas.
Her copper'd bottom casts a softer gleam,
While trembling thro' the green translucent steams.
Along the glassy plane serene she glides,
While azure radiance sparkles on her sides.

Thus the rich vessel moves in trim array;
Like some fair virgin on her bridal day.
Thus, like a swan, she cleaves the wat'ry plain;
The pride and wonder of the liquid main.'*
         FALCONER'S SHIPWRECK, CANTO I.

This charming little poem has a great deal of beauty and
novelty to recommend it. It certainly excells the productions of
the best poets of antiquity, on the subject, inasmuch as the present
naval improvements have exceeded theirs, and the *Albert* of the
SHIPWRECK the *Palinurus* of the AENIS.

'O'er the gay vessel, and her daring band,
Experience'd *Albert* held the chief command
Tho' train'd in boist'rous elements, his mind
Was yet by soft humanity refin'd.
Each joy of wedded love at home he knew;
Abroad, confest the father of his crew!
Brave, liberal, just! The calm domestic scene
Had o'er his temper breath'd a gay serene.
Him science taught, by mystic lore to trace
The planets wheeling in eternal race;

---

* Deviation of arrangement, and verbal alterations were necessary to adapt this
extract to the present occasion.

To mark the ship in floating balance held,
By earth attracted and by seas repel'd;
Or point her devious track, thro' climes unknown,
That leads to every shore in every zone.
He saw the moon thro' heaven's blue concave glide,
And into motion charm th' expanding tide;
While earth impetuous round her axle rolls,
Exalts her watery zone, and sinks the poles.
Light and attraction, from their genial source,
He saw still wand'ring with diminish'd force:
While on the margin of declining day,
Night's shadowy cone reluctant melts away –
Inur'd to peril, with unconquer'd soul,
The chief beheld tempestuous oceans roll;
His genius, ever for th' event prepar'd,
Rose with the storm, and all its dangers shar'd.'

The author's description of his own situation, is particularly impressive.

In order of command,
Succeeds the youngest of our naval band.
But what avails it to record a name
That courts no rank among the sons of fame?
While yet a stripling, oft with fond alarms,
His bosom danc'd to nature's boundless charms.
On him fair science dawn'd, in happier hour,
Awakening into bloom young fancy's flower;
But frowning fortune, with untimely blast,
The blossom wither'd, and the dawn o'ercast.
Forlorn of heart, and by severe decree,
Condemn'd reluctant to the faithless sea,
With long farewel he left the laurel grove,
Where science and the tuneful sisters rove. –

Hither* he wandered, anxious to explore,
Antiquities of nations now no more:
To penetrate each distant realm unknown,
And range excursive o'er th' untravell'd zone.
In vain! – for rude Adversity's command,
Still on the margin of each famous land,
With unrelenting ire, his steps oppos'd;
And every gate of hope against him clos'd! –
Permit my verse, ye blest Pierian train,
To call *Arion*, this ill-fated swain!
For, like that bard unhappy, on his head
Malignant stars their hostile influence shed.
Both, in lamenting numbers, o'er the deep,
With conscious anguish taught the harp to weep:
And both the raging surge in safety bore,
Amid destruction, panting to the shore.
This last our tragic story from the wave
Of dark oblivion haply yet may save:†
With genuine sympathy may yet complain,
While sad remembrance bleeds at every vein.

The technical descriptions are given with great force and beauty, and ('tis said) with equal chastity and correctness; and hence require less aid from poetical fiction; appearing like a "plain, unvarnish'd tale," founded upon realities that occurred under the author's immediate observation. A sea education being deemed so unfavourable to literary pursuits, and, as our author observes, "new to epic lore;" a finished poem from an inhabitant of that element, became still the greater novelty.

While it gives pleasure to every friend to his country, that the education and manners of the British naval officer keep pace with those of her sons on shore; how must the heart dilate, and beat

---

* The Archipelago.

† The ill fated author finally perished on a subsequent voyage to the East Indies.

high, with the idea of his preserving, and, if possible, extending that marked valour, honour and humanity which have been so sacredly handed down to him from his ancestors; and which her enemies so freely confess to be her due? – May they never be separated: for while they remain united, the nation's security, from without, must continue unshaken under the protection of her native bulwark.

St. George's Dock was the third made. It is 250 yards long and 100 broad; comprising an area of 25,300 square yards; with a length of quay of 670 yards. It was constructed at an expence of 21,000l. It is chiefly the resort of West India ships, and is esteemed very commodious.

In passing along the *docks*, the ships of different nations will be discovered by their different construction both in the hulls and rigging; and which will be found to accord with the national character. The *Dutch* ships are strong and square built, mishapen and clumsy; nor, like the natives, has any attempt at the least alteration been ever made in their ornaments or equipment. They are distinguished by a considerable hollowness in the middle, and by the sudden elevation of two square ends; as also by the colossean figure of a head of *Van Trump* or a favourite *Frow*, placed, in contradiction to the custom of other nations, and the order of nature, on the *stern*, upon the *top of the rudder*, with an aspect towards the crew, as if for an *idolatrous* purpose – if a *Dutchman* can be supposed to *adore* any thing but *wealth*. A clumsy mast rises from about the middle of the ship, and a smaller one near the stern; which, altogether, completes a *Dutch dogger*. *Swedish* ships have the same construction and equipment. *French* ships are every way in the opposite extreme; being slightly built; the ornaments tawdry; and the rigging and masts so light and lofty, as to give the idea of *a flying mercury*.

The *English* ships possess a medium between the former; combining strength with beauty and ornament – the *utile* and *dulce* – upon the present improved plan of the *British frigates*. The *Guineamen* here, are in general the handsomest ships; being every way modelled after the *frigates*, and rather more ornamented.

It may be entertaining to the stranger to examine the construction and operation of the [Dock Gates].

Holden's Tide Tables

The Mersey at Liverpool poses a number of navigational problems. Among the more serious are the tidal patterns of the estuary. The mean tidal range of 6.2 metres and the velocity of the tidal currents varying between 4 and 7 knots were very hazardous for sailing ships and the early, underpowered steamships, which were unable to stem the tide. Tidal information in the eighteenth century was scanty and often so inaccurate as to be useless, if not dangerous. Consequently, it is not surprising that the first accurate and reliable tide tables published in Britain were introduced for the Mersey in 1770.

Understanding of tidal mechanisms had developed since Newton's explanation of the influence of gravity. In Europe, some progress had been made in developing methods of tidal prediction Two pioneers, the Swiss, Daniel Benoulli, and the Scot, Colin MacLaurin were to influence the Liverpool project. MacLaurin inspired James Ferguson F.R.S., whose career as a scientific lecturer and demonstrator brought him to Liverpool. There, he became acquainted with William Hutchinson, a former sailor, captain of a privateer, shipowner, boatbuilder, merchant, inventor, author and philanthropist. Appointed Dock Master in 1759, Hutchinson was inspired by Ferguson to record the times and heights of the tide on the dock sill from 1764 until 1793; the first extended survey of tidal data. Richard Holden was a schoolmaster, amateur astronomer and scientist of Castle Street who was acquainted with Ferguson. He and Hutchinson began to devise a method of tidal prediction. It was probably at this point that the lead in the work was assumed by Richard Holden, who brought his brother, George, into the project. Hutchinson was left to continue the observations and data collection.

The Holden dynasty exemplifies the combination of amateur enthusiasm and commercial acuity typical of their generations of Liverpool men. By 1770 the two brothers had compiled a set of tables that they were prepared to publish and the first of the series of 'Holden's Tide Tables' appeared (it was to continue to be published until 1974). The Holdens claimed that their tables were accurate for time by 5 minutes and that predicted heights were correct within seven inches. These claims were probably exaggerated but the tables were so popular that they were adopted as the official tidal information for the port workers. For three generations the Holdens protected their commercial interests by an absolute refusal to divulge their method of prediction. Modern research suggests that they based their calculations on the method devised by Benoulli, with suitable modifications and adjustments.

The involvement of the family in the production and publishing of the tables began with the two brothers, Richard and George. They were not Liverpool men by birth but originated in the area of Lonsdale on the Lancashire–Yorkshire border. Little is known of Richard's career before he appears as a schoolmaster in Liverpool but his will shows that he had a great interest in mathematics and science. George was a master at Bentham school before taking holy orders and accepting, in 1758, a post as curate of Pilling on the northwest Lancashire coast. In 1767 he gave up the living and returned to Bentham, where he served as curate of Tatham Fell chapel. George's son, also named George, after graduating from the University of Glasgow, became the curate of Horton in Ribblesdale, not far from his home in Bentham and later succeeded his father at Tatham until 1820. His son, the third George, was a Glasgow graduate and, after experience in Yorkshire, became the perpetual curate of the ancient chapel of St Andrew at Maghull, now a northern suburb of Liverpool. He was, perhaps, more concerned with his involvement in the family business than his religious duties but the vicarage he built and the chapel he served still exist adjacent to the later church at Maghull. His portrait adorned the Tables until the twentieth century.

DOCK GATES.

Turning along the north end of St. George's Dock, we come to the *gates* of that entrance. At or soon after high water, the gates are shut, and, of course, remain so till opened by the next flood tide. In each gate will be perceived an opening, which, at high tides, is intended to evacuate the water in the dock to a certain quantity necessary for floating the ships, thereby avoiding risk from any unnecessary pressure of water upon the gates. For better security, two pair of gates were thought advisable here, although one pair is found sufficient. In very high tides, when these openings are not sufficient, other sluices can be opened below, by machinery contrived for that purpose. There is yet another intention these openings answer; which is, that at spring tides, when the tides begin regularly to fall or become lower each tide, if the water left within the dock were at any time above the level of the succeeding tide at high water, the gates could not be got open. The *dock-gate-men*, are therefore furnished with a table, descriptive of every succeeding height of tide, and regulate that of the dock accordingly. An annual tide table is published by MR HOLDEN, which ascertains the times of *high water*, and the *heights* the *tides flow*, with an accuracy before unknown, and in a method yet a secret with his family. Why not purchased by the public, at any price, if it will apply to all parts of the coast of the kingdom? The management of the dock gates is submitted to the care of four men, two on each side, who assist in opening and shutting them, in the manner that may be observed; and who, with the *dock master*, also assist in directing the ships through the gates.

The arched construction, and the position of the gates, are well calculated to resist the vast pressure of water which they have to sustain. The butments of the gates are formed of stones of large dimensions, so bound together, or cramped, with iron, as to form a body sufficiently compact and heavy to support the lateral pressure of the gates; which latter are proportionally strong, without being heavy or clumsy. The gates move backward and forward on iron rollers, upon a sill at the bottom; and have no perpendicular pressure to bear, except their own weight. These gates are 25 feet high, and 38 feet wide. The *average* rise of the tides at these gates, at spring tides, is about 21 feet; and 12 feet at neap tides. The *highest* rise of the tide at the Dublin dock, does not exceed 13 feet.

OBSERVATIONS ON THE DOCKS.

The rapidity of the tides in the river, and exposure to strong westerly winds, must have been very unfavourable to the accommodation of shipping both in the river and the more interior harbour, or *pool*, as it was then named; so that so early as in 1561, attempts were made at something like a dock, as a shelter from storms; but it was not till about 75 years ago, that Parliament was applied to for an act to build a regular dock; since which time the docks have increased in number with the increase and flourishing state of the town, and are now augmented to thirteen: five wet docks; five graving docks; and three dry docks; (independent of the Duke of Bridgewater's dock) occupying a space of about three miles in circumference; the whole constructed, formed and built upon the bed of the river. Its is to be observed, that George's, the Old, and Salthouse Dock, communicate, so that ships can pass from one to the other, and into the graving docks, without going into the river, where their being unmanned or unrigged might expose them to injury from the wind and tide in so doing. The King's and Queen's Dock communicate together in the same manner, and with their own graving docks.

There are perfect communications under ground between all the *wet docks*, by large tunnels, for the purpose of one dock cleaning or washing another; so that when a dock is to be cleaned (as they are all very subject to fill with mud) and which is generally done once a year; it is left dry at low water, by keeping the gates open; the sluices are opened into it in difference directions; and a great number of men enter it, who, with spades, shovel the mud into the currents made by the sluices, till the dock becomes sufficiently cleared, and which usually occupies a space of some weeks. Flat-bottomed boats are also employed at these times for loading the carrying out the mud, which they discharge into the river. The *dry docks* are cleared from mud in the same manner, by sluices opened from their respective wet docks.

The docks have Watch, Scavengers and Lamps, distinct from those of the town; and fires are not suffered, and even candles not permitted to be lighted on board the ships, except secured in lanthorns, nor tobacco smoaked, under a penalty of 40s.; nor any combustible matter left on the decks or on the adjoining quays in the night, under a fine of 10l. By these precautions, an accident from fire (so much to be dreaded) has, fortunately, not happened: and yet scarce a week passes without fines being incurred for these practices. The penalty for having gunpowder on board in the docks, in 40s.

Large ships, when loaded, cannot pass the dock gates at neap tides for want of a sufficient height of water there; so that, when a ship of that description, in the dock, is ready for sea during the spring tides, and the wind unfair, it is conveyed into the river and there remains at anchor, to take the advantage of a favourable wind. If a ship arrive from sea during neap tides, it continues in the same situation till the next spring tides rise high enough to float it into the dock.

The construction of the docks is not only laborious and expensive, but tedious; arising from the magnitude and weight of the materials of which they are formed, and the interruptions given by the returns of the tides, their currents and the swell of the sea in stormy weather. The quality of the stone used in the structure of the docks, contributes essentially in their formation; as no other materials could so securely bind, connect, support and mound the whole.

The dock dues, paid for the entrance of ships were

	l.	s.	d.
In 1724	810	11	6
1776	5,064	10	10
1786	7,508	0	1
1796	12,377	7	7
1797	13,319	12	8

which gives some idea of the progressive extension of the trade of the town.

The annual expences attending the docks, are, according to the last year's statement ending 24ᵗʰ June, as follow.

	l.	s.	d.
Dock gatemen	636	15	0
Dock watchmen	1,763	12	10
Incidents	219	10	9
Surveyor	52	10	0
Engineer	100	0	0
Harbour Master	73	10	0
Five dock masters, at 105l. each	525	0	0
Two deputy do.	72	16	0
Water bailiff	50	0	0
Tide Tables	10	10	0
Smiths work, &c.	175	9	6
Cordage, tar, paint, etc.	113	19	6
Parish taxes	465	19	0
Lamps lighting	176	16	0
Treasurer's commission and Clerks salaries	665	19	7
	5,102	8	7

Thus the annual income and expenditure of the docks may be nearly ascertained. The original and present construction of the docks and piers, have incurred a debt of, at present, 113,419l. 2s. by money borrowed upon them, as upon turnpikes, under different Acts of Parliament. The direction, etc. of the docks is vested in the corporation, as trustees; whose accounts are annually examined and settled by seven commissioners, not of the body corporate, appointed for the purpose.

Liverpool's Trade during the Eighteenth Century

As we have seen, the development of Liverpool was founded on certain geographical, economic, historical, and geopolitical advantages. In his account of the dock system, Moss outlines the trade using the particular basins and this gives a good starting point for an analysis of the trading and shipping interests of the town in the last decade of the century. It is easy to assume that the commerce of the town revolved around the African trade, but this is a misapprehension. In 1771, 323 voyages were made from the port to other destinations, involving a total tonnage of 35,586, against 106 sailing to Africa of 10,929 tons. The same source (*Essay Towards the History of Liverpool* W. Enfield 1773) gives a list of the cargoes which were exported to the various destinations. The commodities range from bricks for Antigua, worsted caps for Barbados, red herrings for the settlers on Dominica, oats for Grenada, Irish muffins for Jamaica, haberdashery for St Kitts and apothecary's ware to Montserrat.

The other destinations listed include Newfoundland, Nova Scotia, New England, New York, Philadelphia and the other American colonies. Liverpool ships sailed to the Baltic and the Mediterranean carrying goods as varied as alum, bricks, copper, mustard, chests of drawers, stationery-goods and salt. These varied and mixed cargoes became known in the records of the custom service as a 'Liverpool Cargo'. For example the *Bridget* of 150 tons, on one voyage, carried barrels of salt beef, firkins of butter, barrels of herrings, boxes of candles, 3 trunks, casks of hams, refined sugar, bottled beer, lime, coils of rope, six thousand bricks, puncheons of rum and 20 kegs of tripe. No wonder that one historian of Liverpool's trade in the eighteenth century entitled his article *Shoes, and Ships and Sealing Wax*.

Great impetus was given to trade with the overseas possessions of the Crown by the Navigation Acts. These pieces of legislation dating from 1650 until 1696 were solely intended to encourage trade and, especially, the sea-borne carriage of goods in English ships. It was laid down that colonial goods were only to be carried in English ships or on colonial ships with a predominantly English crew. Originally designed to injure the universal cargo-carrying trade of the Dutch, the laws were extended to prohibit the carriage of certain colonial commodities, except in English ships. These laws were not repealed until the mid-nineteenth century. This policy, known as 'Mercantilism', was adopted by many nations. The mother country was to have the monopoly of the carriage of the goods, both imports and exports, from and to their Plantations, as colonies were known. As foreign trade became economically more important, governments were urged by the mercantile and commercial interests of their countrymen to pursue ever more restrictive trade regulation.

Amongst other benefits of the navigation laws to Liverpool was the encouragement of ship building. The criterion for qualifying ships for colonial trade was that they should be British built, even if they were subsequently owned by colonial merchants. It was not only the hulls which were exported but the sails, rigging and tackle. The demand from the colonies was an important stimulus to the textile trade. The Plantations were excellent markets for cloth, manufactured clothing and for shoes and other tanned leather items. The dominating growth of the cotton industry in Lancashire was, in part, stimulated by the demands of the colonists, which were met by the Liverpool merchants. Although other goods were used for trade in Africa, notably iron and other pieces of metal work, the list of commodities given by Enfield shows the overwhelming importance of fabrics – including the re-export of Indian-made light cotton cloths – as trade goods to be exchanged with African potentates in return for slaves.

Liverpool and Privateers

That Liverpool provided a haven from the European privateers in the Channel waters was an important factor in the evolution of the port. The ship owners of Liverpool soon realised that this was a game in which they could profitably participate. The most common name for these vessels was Privateer but they were sometimes known as Letters of Marque. In time of war it was customary for European governments to issue licences (Letters of Marque) which enabled their merchant vessels to take enemy shipping and to profit from the sale of the cargo and the vessel itself, so-called prize money. The holding of a Letter of Marque and Reprisal was what distinguished the legitimate private man of war from the pirate. Privateers were divided into two types. There were those armed merchant ships which obtained a licence and, while conducting their normal business, might make use of it to seize any target of opportunity. There were also ships fitted out and intended for the capture and destruction of the enemy's commerce. Prize money was their aim and intention. The latter category were built, armed and manned like smaller warships – frigate and sloops – of the Royal Navy. Liverpool Letters of Marque varied very much in size and armaments. In 1778 the ships sailing from Liverpool ranged in size from the *Lady Granby* of 45 tons to the *Mersey* of 1,400 tons. Together they mounted 1,626 guns and were manned by about 6,500 sailors. A purpose-built privateer needed to be a good sea boat, fast, well-armed and with accommodation for a large crew so that there were sufficient men to provide prize crews for captured vessels.

It was during the War of the Austrian Succession (1740–48) that Liverpool first seems to have sent privateers to sea, four vessels are recorded in 1744. During this war, it was Captain Fortunatus Wright who emerged as the pre-eminent Liverpool privateer commander in the *St George* During the Seven Years War and the American War, Liverpool ships ranged the seas in search of prey. Some were highly successful but none more so than the *Mentor*. Rejected by her original owners as unseaworthy, her builder sent her to sea, under the command of Captain Dawson. In October 1778 she captured the French East Indiaman, *Carnatic* with a cargo valued at £135,000. Dawson married the owner's daughter, left the sea and became a shipbuilder. The *Mentor* foundered off Newfoundland in 1782 with the loss of 31 lives.

In the 1793 war with France, Liverpool again began to man and fit out privateers. However, the campaign began with a disaster. On 20 March 1793, the newly launched, *Pelican* of 20 guns and with a complement of 100, was on display. Crowded with shareholders, their wives and families, she sailed up and down the river opposite the Pier Head. Off Seacombe, the vessel suddenly healed over, water poured through the open gun ports and she sank in moments. Seventy or eighty passengers and crew were drowned. For many years the topmasts of the ship stood above the water. Only a few days after this disaster the *Harriet* brought in the first prize of the war, *L'Agreable* loaded with sugar worth £10,000. The Liverpool privateers continued to cruise against enemy shipping and achieved some remarkable successes. It has to be remembered that there were also considerable losses of ships, men and material. For example, on 9 November 1808 the ships *Lydia* and *Lord Cranstoun* were both captured with their crews of 96 English and 12 Portuguese sailors.

It is difficult to assess the strategic and tactical value of the *guerre de corse*. While the privateers provided an auxiliary support for the Royal Navy by imposing a commercial blockade, they also were great consumers of materials, resources and men. Certainly, the privateers provided a reservoir of excellent and belligerent seamen who might be recruited into the navy and often unemployed or cashiered naval officers could find berths aboard the Letters of Marque.

The LIVERPOOL DOCKS possess magnitude, convenience and a harmony of parts, unrivalled throughout the world. Necessity first prompted the measure, and the spirit of the town has, by no very small degrees, brought them to their present state of perfection, and induced a desire in the metropolis to copy after them.

So novel a scene, as the docks present, must greatly interest the attention of the contemplative stranger, and fill the mind with a degree of pleasure and astonishment, he has not before experienced from a similar cause; and which even anticipation does not much abate. While the general observer contemplates the whole with amazement; the more discriminating merchant regards it with an additional gratification, derived from the great resulting advantages to commerce which await it.

The surprise of the stranger, on first crossing any of the dock gates at low water, (especially the old dock or salt-house dock) and without having passed them at high water, will be not a little excited by observing so large a number of ships afloat, so far removed from the river and so much elevated above its surface: the mind, if unprepared for it, will for a moment discredit the external sense, and fluctuate between deception and reality. At all times of the tide, it is interesting to observe, that such a number

Press warrant

This authorisation was granted
to Captain Pasley of the sloop
Weasal on 19 September 1770. It
delegates the implementation
of the warrant to Acting
Lieutenant Lord Cochrane.
Alexander Cochrane (9th
Earl of Dundonald) had an
unusual career in the Royal;
Navy. After reaching the
rank of Acting Lieutenant,
he became disenchanted
with the service as a result
of a voyage to Guinea.
He left the sea and took a
commission in the 104th
Regiment, but he soon
resigned from the army
and devoted the rest of his
life to chemical research.
Though this was ultimately
useful he reduced the
family to penury in the
process. His son was
to find naval fame as
Thomas, Lord Cochrane
(10th Earl of Dundonald).

of ships should be so regularly and orderly disposed, surrounded
by houses in the heart of the town, and there as securely placed
as any other property in any other situation. The seaman here
can step into and out of his ship, with as much ease as he passes
the threshold of the door of his house; and can pass from one
to the other, with as much facility as he can visit his next door
neighbour. That valuable character, the British sailor, is little
observed in time of war; as when in port, he is under the necessity
of secreting himself from the impress. Much to the credit of those
who have had the direction of that service *here*, during the latter
part of the present war, this painful, yet indispensable, task has
been conducted with a decorum unusual in former wars. The late
adopted mode of levying men for the navy has, no doubt, greatly
precluded the necessity of pressing.

The advantages a wet dock possesses over every kind of port
or harbour, are very great. The ships cannot possibly be affected
by any kind of weather; they always are afloat; can lade and
unlade, at all times, without any obstacle or risk of injury to the
cargoes. The docks, here, are so compacted, and contiguous to
every requisite for the equipment of the ships, that every possible
delay is prevented; and finally, from their contiguity with the
warehouses, &c. the ships can be loaded and discharged with
dispatch and at the trifling expence, under the immediate eye of
the merchant.

Hawks Abroad!

One of the abiding eighteenth century legends is of the ruffianly press
gang, sent by a captain to roam the streets of a port, snatching up the
innocent passer-by for brutal service in the Royal Navy. This is the
antithesis of the 'Hearts of Oak', 'jolly tar' naval heroes of Nelson. The
powers to impress for service in both the army and the navy dated from
the reign of Edward I and are un-repealed today. Part of the myth is that
the eighteenth century navy was almost entirely manned by men with no
sea experience, swept up by the press gang and carried off for service.
In fact, a large proportion of the sailors of the navy were men who had

volunteered, often a successful captain could almost fill his ship with experienced sailors who received a £70 bounty. For the rest of the men they relied on other sources. Each county or town was required to find a given number of men for the Navy. These so-called 'quota men' were usually found from the gaols and ne'r-do-wells of the community and were sometimes men who accepted service as a commutation of capital sentences. The third source of recruits was provided by the Impress Service, a branch of the Royal Navy. Their task was to forcibly recruit men and again, despite the legends, their main targets were seamen or men with some experience afloat. Common sense suggests that no captain wanted a crew of novices.

Press gangs could be of two sorts. Some were launched by an individual ship. A desperate captain would send off boats to raid either returning merchantmen – ships outward bound were exempt – or small ports and harbours. Sailors in the merchant navy were reluctant to enter the Royal Navy, not because of the danger or the harsh conditions – merchant ships were little better – but because of the difference in pay. On the other hand, prize money was a strong incentive and once men were taken by the press they often accepted their inevitable fate and volunteered, hoping to obtain promotion and preferential pay.

Most press gangs came from the Impress Service which, after 1793, had permanent establishments in 51 ports. These were organised into 31 districts. At each of the ports a Lieutenant would be stationed at a 'Rendezvous', usually an inn where they had a secure room for their 'recruits' before transfer to the 'Press Tender', a small vessel. When a tender was full, the men would be taken to one of the receiving ships, a superannuated ship of the line converted into a hulk (the 'Princess' was anchored in the Mersey). There the men would be medically examined and awaited their allocation to a ship.

Many Liverpool seamen were caught in the so-called 'Hot Press of 1794' when sailings from Liverpool were embargoed as the Navy prepared for the French war. At that time, the gangs raided markets and fairs in inland towns. They even stopped the mail coaches and seized men out of them. It was common practice to press men intensively when a particular danger threatened or at a time of naval expansion. In 1805 – Trafalgar year – forty Irishmen were seized as they disembarked at Liverpool from the Dublin packet, though most were subsequently released.

The press was hated by seamen but also by the local citizens. The warning 'Hawks Abroad!' put everyone on the defensive and seamen sought safe hiding places. The town authorities were opposed to the press because it was seen as liable to disrupt trade and lead to violence and riot. To try to minimise its effects the Corporation of Liverpool offered bounties of two guineas to recruits who volunteered. That this did not always have the desired effect is shown by the events of 1780 when a detachment tried to seize a small group of sailors from the house kept by James Richards in Hackins Hey. One of the defenders was shot dead and Richards wounded. The dead man was buried in St Peter's Churchyard, his grave stone is preserved in Walton Park Cemetery. In October 1793 an attempt to seize Captain McIlroy of the sloop *Anna* ended with the Captain shot dead and a riot that wrecked the rendezvous on Strand Street.

Crossing the *dock gates* (after high water) we proceed along the east side of George's dock. Passing along the arcade of the handsome and convenient warehouses which now present, we discover, behind them, a range of other *warehouses*, some of which are so *high*, that they might be viewed with surprise by a native of Edinburgh. They are designed, chiefly, as storehouses for corn. At the other end of these building, is the town prison: of very ancient date; and which belonged formerly to the Derby family, and used by them as a residence – what a scope for reflection! – Looking up the street on the right (Water-street), we discover the Exchange; from whence we commenced our *ramble*.

The line, from hence, in the direction of north and south, was originally the boundary of the river.

The narrow passage on the lower side of the prison, leads to the Old Church yard; the lower part of which affords a pleasant walk, as it presents a desirable opening into the river, through the gut of St. George's dock bason. At the south end of this walk, is the Merchants Coffee House, where the newspapers are read; and where lodgings may be had by those who prefer the situation. Cannon were formerly planted here, for the defence of the harbour. This lower part of the Church yard was raised from the shore, less than fifty years ago; as originally the base of the tower of the church was washed by the river.

Going off at the opposite end of the church yard, we pass between a boat builder's yard on the right, and a ship builder's yard on the left; either of which may be viewed. We then arrive at a small *glasshouse*, for the manufacture of flint glass; and the turn from thence to the left, leads to the *public Baths*; they are distinct for ladies and gentlemen, are esteemed commodious and elegant, and may be viewed. The road father on, presents the *Fort*, which, with its formidable artillery, promise an ample security against any enemy's ships that may attempt an entrance into the harbour. A strong guard of soldiers is always kept here. It is open for public recreation. The soldiers are commonly exercised and the guard relieved, every evening. A very advantageous view down the river, is obtained here, and from whence the *rock point* may be very distinctly observed. The ride along this shore, for some miles, is very pleasant, especially in warm weather; as it will be found very cool and refreshing, with a westerly wind particularly. Two roads branch off, inland, at one and three miles distance, along the shore: the first, at Beacon-gutter: and the second at Bootle mills, where accommodations for bathing, lodging &c. as at other watering places, may be had at two good houses.

Liverpool at War

In his *Guide*, Dr Moss gives little intimation that he is writing in a time of war. Hostilities with the new French Republic began 1 February 1793, thus inaugurating a struggle which continued, with one short break, until June 1815. Earlier wars had led to the erection of defensive batteries, the largest of which was at the foot of the churchyard of St Nicholas Church. This had become redundant with the building of George's Dock which blocked its field of fire. Consequently, in 1778, when John Paul Jones was cruising in the Irish Sea, a new battery was erected on a promontory known as Hog's Hey Nook, slightly to the north of church. This fort, which could accommodate a garrison of 100 men, was eventually built at the cost of the Corporation.

North Shore

This area, north of Leeds Street, was a popular place for sea bathing. The
bathing machines, owned by the Van Dries family provided changing facilities
and, when dragged into the sea, allowed the cautious bather to enter the water
unobserved. In this picture the North Shore mill can be seen nearest the
foreground while the more distant windmill is adjacent to a stile known as
'The Wishing Gate' which was the point from which the families of seafarers
waved their last farewells. For their convenience an inn of the same name stood
close by.

In addition, a regiment of foot, *The Liverpool Blues*, was raised and
placed at the King's service by the town. The new fort was ready for
use by 1781 and comprised a *demi-lune*, or half-moon battery, barracks
and store. The 20 guns commanded the river. The entrance to the fort
was opposite Dennison Street and the gates were flanked by piers, one
carved with a lion and the other bearing the Liver Bird of the town.

The war with France, in 1793, brought a new threat of naval
attacks and invasion. The fort was put in order and outworks
constructed. A troop of yeomanry cavalry and a battery of artillery
were recruited from amongst the townspeople. Additionally, two
regiments of volunteers were raised in the town, one known as the
Royal Liverpool Blues, the other as *The Royal Liverpool Volunteers*. Though

gorgeously uniformed, the regiments were never to be put to the test of battle.

There was considerable alarm in 1797 when a small French force landed in west Wales at Fishguard. The Mayor and Corporation of Liverpool took steps to defend the town. The pilot cutters were sent out to scout for the approaching invasion fleet, powder and ammunition were collected and placed in the fort and other magazines. Twenty guns, both 32 and 18 pounders, were mounted in the fort. Ten more 18 pounders were set in additional batteries to protect the docks and guard commanding points on the river. The Corporation supplied the guns and the Admiralty were asked to provide two 44 gun ships to guard the river, though it is unlikely that these ever arrived. In the meantime, the army of French criminals and Irish renegades had surrendered to the Welsh yeomanry cavalry. According to legend, they mistook the Welsh women in their tall black hats and red cloaks for a regiment of infantry. By 1799 the Corporation were rather regretting their lavish expenditure on defences and made moves to obtain a contribution from the Government, an objective in which they ultimately failed.

However, the Corporation were undeterred from action when, in 1803, a French invasion by Napoleon seemed inevitable. At a meeting on 18 July, a committee was formed to put the town in a defensible state. A plan of defences, drawn up by Major General Benson, was adopted as 'excellently calculated for the purpose for the defence of the harbour'. It involved erecting four new batteries, one of nine guns at the Red Noses, eight were to be mounted at Hog's Nook, a further seven at King's Dock and five at George's Dock. About £3,000 was immediately allocated to fund this work, though it was calculated that the ultimate cost would amount to £11,530. In order to stiffen the command of the Liverpool area, Prince Fredrick of Gloucester was appointed to command the north west district and he made his headquarters at St Domingo House in Everton. On his arrival, the Prince sought the Corporation's help in providing barracks for the additional garrison. Cunningly, the Corporation built, on a site near the gaol, a barrack block capable of conversion into fifteen houses. The new barracks cost £8,076 but were profitably let to the army for a period of seven years at an annual rent of £1,500. Patriotism did not have to interfere with business! Untested by the enemy, the fort

The Tower of Liverpool

Originally built as the town house of the Stanley family the tower received a licence to crenelate in 1406, though its fortifications were intended more for effect than serious military use. It seems to have been used from the sixteenth century as a gaol. Following the execution of Lord Derby after the Civil War, the tower was bought by Alexander Greene in 1653. It was recovered by the Derby family after the Restoration and leased to Thomas Clayton, a prominent Liverpool merchant. It was still partially used as a gaol for prisoners in 1715. In 1737 the Corporation leased the tower from its owner and while the lower floors housed the prisoners, the upper floors were used as a banqueting and assembly rooms.

succumbed to natural forces and by 1813 was very dilapidated. Later, another fort was built to the north, while the old fortifications were swallowed up in dock expansions. Liverpool's war was fought at sea and its home defences remained untested against the 'Corsican Tyrant'.

John Howard and Liverpool Gaol

The fame of John Howard (1726–1790) as a prison reformer has, to some extent, been eclipsed by the activities of Elizabeth Fry (1780–1845), but earlier in the century he had roused social consciousness about the conditions under which prisoners were kept. He became the acknowledged European authority who was widely consulted on the design and management of prisons. Born in Stoke Newington of well-to-do parents, in 1726, Howard, like many other philanthropists of the period, was associated with the radical, non-conformist church. In 1755 he sailed to Lisbon to view the destruction caused by the great earthquake. The ship was captured and Howard gained experience of prison life during two years incarceration. In 1773, as High Sheriff of Bedfordshire, he inspected the county prisons and was horrified by the conditions he found. For the next seventeen years Howard travelled extensively in Britain and the Continent gathering information on prisons. He talked and wrote copiously on the subject before his death on a fact finding mission to Turkey.

In Liverpool, in Moss' time, the ancient tower contained the gaol. Dating from the 15th century, it provided totally unsuitable accommodation for felons and debtors. It was not even secure and in 1753 orders were given to raise and repair the walls. By the following year, the dilapidation was even worse and the town clerk offered a generous reward for the recapture of two men and a woman who had escaped. In 1774 the Corporation purchased the freehold of the tower and ordered enlargement and repairs. However, in February 1777, a committee was set up which ordered an architect, John Hope, to prepare plans for a gaol based on the design of London's recently rebuilt Newgate prison. It is probably no accident that John Howard was in the town at this time and in April of that year he was asked to give advice 'about the gaol of this town ... altering and conducting the better economy thereof'. In return he was given the freedom of the borough. He had previously visited the tower which he described as 'out of repair, close and very dirty'. On later visits in 1779 and 1782 he reported some improvement in conditions.

In 1784 the Grand Jury utterly condemned the inadequacy of the tower gaol and plans were put in hand for the building of a prison. Two fields near the canal terminus were purchased as the site for the new gaol. Work was very slow and in 1793, before the new building had been put into use, it was allocated for the accommodation of 4,000 prisoners of war. This was initially thought to be a temporary expedient but proved to be a long term arrangement. In 1799 the council demanded an increase in rent from the Commissioners of Transport, who were responsible for the holding of war prisoners.

Liverpool protested that the French had damaged the building and that the town was forced to continue using the totally unsuitable tower. A report of 1803 describes the old gaol as filthy, with a large dunghill in the middle of the yard. For felons there were seven dungeons, each six feet square and ten feet underground, while an eighth had a square grated window on to the street. It was not until 1811 that the new prison was cleared of prisoners of war and allocated to those for whom it had been designed.

The gaol had a high perimeter wall and gate house. Inside, a central block had six radiating wings. In his 'Picture of Liverpool' of 1793, Dr Moss was less kind than in the present work. He writes '... on a fair calculation [it] will hold half the inhabitants of Liverpool. It is the remark of a French wit that a prison always looks best from the outside. This idea seems to have influenced the Corporation, for such is the external appearance, that a distant view indicates a magnificent castle. The pile is enormous, the materials of which it is composed would build a village. An impartial observer must be divided in opinion whether it is more deserving of ridicule or reprobation'. Forty years later a new gaol was built in the suburb of Walton. It is significant of Howard's relationship with Liverpool, where he had advised on the design of the new gaol, that the street in which it stood was named 'Great Howard Street'.

Turning up *Denison-street*, behind the Fort, will be discovered, from the top of the street, on the left, the *New Prison*; so immensely large, that, for the sake of suffering humanity, it is to be hoped it will never be filled; except with its present description of inhabitants – *French prisoners* – who, fortunately for themselves, were here preserved from the famine and bloodshed that so desolated their native country: for the honour of *this*, they have been favoured with every comfort and indulgence their situation will admit of, and even, on most occasions, to the extent which their natural levity solicits.

The situation of the prison is healthful, and it has many conveniences; yet on examination, it will be observed, that the *debtor*, whatever his constitution, habits and health may be, cannot

The Old Hall by Matthew Gregson

The Moore family had been amongst the most prominent of the Liverpool citizens since the Middle Ages when they had served as members of the Corporation, Mayors and as Members of Parliament. Their original home was Moore Hall or the Old Hall, as it was known in the eponymous street. In the thirteenth century they acquired rights in Kirkdale and built a new house, Bank Hall. In the Civil War period Sir John Moore was one of the most prominent of the Lancashire parliamentarians and a judge at the trial of King Charles. Consequently, their influenced declined after the Restoration and in the early eighteenth century they left the area. The Old Hall in its later years served as a dower house before, as we see it here, being broken up into tenements prior to its demolition in the early nineteenth century.

be accommodated with a more favourable *cell* to sleep in, than the hardiest and most abandoned *felon*. Such, at least, seems to be the original intention; is so, 'tis "devoutly to be wished" that it may be varied. – It is capable of lodging the inhabitants of all the prisons in the kingdom, northward.

Close by the prison are, a steam mill for rolling and slitting of iron; a white lead work; and two Manufactories of ashes, from soap lees. – Brick-kilns are numerous.

Returning the way we came, the head of the Leeds and Wigan canal presents; on which an elegant Packet boat passes from hence to Wigan, every morning (except Sunday) at eight, and arrives there at six o'clock; and another from thence sets off at six, and arrives here at four. The Fares; 3s. and 2s. The right bank of the Canal affords a very pleasant walk; but is inaccessible, from dirt and the parsimony of the *proprietors*, in wet weather; and there is no carriage way. – The quantity of coal imported by this canal, from Wigan, &c. for the supply of the town, and the export to the different parts of Europe, America, and the West Indies, is considerable: hence Liverpool may be called a coal port. About 100 flats are employed for the purpose, of 42 tons each, and each drawn by one horse; which makes three passages in two weeks. A variety of other boats are employed for commercial purposes. A coal flat with a full load of limestones, &c. in return, will drag after it, afloat in the canal, a raft containing 9000 feet of fir timber, weighing 180 tons; which altogether makes a weight of 222 tons drawn by one horse.

From the head of the canal, is an opening to *St. Paul's church*. Howsoever the church yard and body of the church may pass for a miniature of the original, the dome and cupola serve but to remind us of *their* inferiority. Being on elevated ground, the dome has a good effect, at a distance; but there is no station near, from whence the whole can be viewed to any advantage.

Turning towards the river, we come to a narrow and very dirt [*sic*] street, called *Oldhall-street*; in the narrowest and dirtiest part of which, four streets meet, and which once formed one of the markets of the town, in its primitive state. In this market place stood a *Cross* (as is still usual in many market towns) which was called the *White Cross*. This narrow street and the adjoining ones, formed what was considered the most genteel part of the town, thirty years ago. On advancing nearer the Exchange, we soon get extricated from the dirt and difficulties of a narrow street, by the opening which has been made, and which is meant to be extended farther, for the public accommodation. A very superb Cross, formerly stood where the Exchange is now placed.

From what has been observed, it will appear, that the north extremity of the town is so circumstanced, at present, as not to admit of much improvement in building.

Southeast view of the Liverpool Infirmary, 1770

The Infirmary was built in 1743 from the proceeds of a subscription set up by the 'clergy, physicians, surgeons and merchants' which raised £1,456 14s. 9d. toward its costs. The building was erected on Oil Mill Fields and comprised a central block with two wings for 'decayed seamen and their wives'. It opened on 25 March 1749 with a staff of three physicians, three surgeons and a number of servants and nurses, under the control of a matron who received a salary of £6. Nurses were instructed to 'behave with tenderness to the patients, with submission to superiors, with courtesy and respect to all strangers'. When this engraving was made the original building had been enlarged and improved.

SURVEY OF THE TOWN CONTINUED.

The *Hotel*, at the bottom of Lord-street, from its central situation, will now be the best station for the stranger to recommence his ramble from. Going up *Church-street*, opposite the Church, we turn into *Tarleton-street*; which leads to *Williamson-square*; wherein will be observed, by the King's Arms in front, at the farther side, the Theatre; which may be entered behind, by a door under the stage.

At the upper end, *Houghton-street* leads into *Clayton-square*; which presents a regularity not to be found in the squares we have already passed. It was the last built, and may afford a specimen of the improving taste of the town. Passing through the opposite opening, we are in *Ranelagh-street*; and turning up, we pass a *ropery*, where ropes, cables, and the various rigging of a ship, are made. To the left of the top of this street, in *Bolton-street* (dirty and unpaved) are very elegant fresh water *baths*; cold, temperate and warm; for ladies and gentlemen, distinctly. They are supplied from the well of the adjoining cotton manufactory, that is worked by a steam engine.

Retracing our steps, we cross *Ranelagh Place*, and proceed up *Mount Pleasant*,* till we come to *Clarence-street*, on the left; which leads to a spacious road that directs us farther up the hill to the *Poor House*: the front of which is chiefly applied to working and eating rooms; and the two extended back wings, to dwelling apartments for the poor.

Continuing the direction; we perceive the buildings before us, on the right; called *Edge-hill*. Asscending [*sic*] the summit of the rising ground, the road on the right leads to the very pleasant villages of Wa'tree, Childwall and Woolon.

Keeping upon the summit of the hill to the left, we pass the venerable remains of *Vernon-hall*; not the less distinguished by its stately pines; and immediately cross the great south road at the village of *Low-hill*; which formerly was a fashionable, and the only, retreat of the town inhabitants for recreation. Crossing another road, in the same direction, at a pleasant villa, we approach the village of *Everton*; which passing through, we yet cross another road, and arrive finally at *St. Domingo*. A house was built here, and the adjoining grounds purchased, with the product of a French prize ship from St. Domingo, in a former war, and hence so called. A new house is now erected, which possesses much elegance.

As this situation terminates the ridge of the hill, it presents a fine extended prospect of the adjoining country before us, to the north and east. The sudden breaking in upon the sea, has a

---

* In rising this street, the dome of St Paul's appears to great advantage.

wonderful effect, at high water. – The whole line of the summit we have traced, affords good and varied views of the town, river and sea.

Performing a retrograde motion; at the first turn to the right, we descend towards the lower part of the village. This descent offers a very charming display of the river and sea, with the town below. Passing several elegant houses, we arrive at the road which leads down towards the town; and where an advantageous view of the east side of the town is obtained. Adjoining, is a coffee house, where every accommodation of tea, dinners, &c. and lodging may be had. Descending, we come to *Richmond*, where a *woollen hall* (of no great celebrity) is occasionally open. The back view to Everton, during this descent, has a pleasing effect. *St. Ann-street*, facing *St. Ann's Church*, is a street of much elegance, which is not diminished by *Trinity Church* towards the south end. St. Ann's church has a good effect from hence. The first turn on the right out of St. Ann-street, leads to the *Circus*; where are elegant livery stables, and where equestrian exercises are occasionally performed by Astley and others. A little farther, we discover, on the right, an uniform row of houses, called *Islington*;* facing which is the *Infirmary*, which, with its side colonades, has somewhat the form of the Queen's palace. The neat buildings on each side of the Infirmary, in front, are dwellings for the widows of seamen.

Liverpool's Churches

Ecclesiastically, Liverpool remained a Chapelry of St Mary, Walton, until 1699. However, long before – no date is known – a chapel dedicated to St Mary del Key (quay) had been established. In 1361 a further chapel of St Nicholas had been founded, situated on the waterfront adjacent to St Mary's. As the wealth of the town grew, St Nicholas Chapel was graced with a white statue of the Virgin and designated as a place of pilgrimage by the Pope. It also acquired four chantry

---

* The stranger will have discovered a tendency here to ape the London names of places, but which is to be feared will, on comparison, tend to lessen in his estimation what he might otherwise have considered as neat or commodious.

St Nicholas' church

The church depicted in these drawings is the building as it was at the time of Dr Moss' writing. In 1774 the old nave, which dated from *c.* 1360 and aisles, added in the late seventeenth century, had been pulled down and replaced by a structure in the 'Gothick' style. The ancient tower was left standing and in 1746 a wooden spire had been erected on it, to enhance the church tower's usefulness as a navigational mark. One of the first batteries erected to protect the entrance to the port was located in front of the churchyard. The gabled building in the foreground of both these views was what the remained of the older chapel of St Mary which had served as a school, a boathouse, an inn and a warehouse. It was demolished in 1814.

chapels, one of which served as a school. These – including the chapel of St Mary – disappeared after the Chantries Act of Edward VI (1547). During Tudor times, the patronage of the church was assumed by the Corporation. A growing population and the inflation of civic pride made the old arrangements untenable and, in 1699, at the petition of the Corporation, Liverpool was created an independent parish. The arrangements were highly unusual. A new church was to be built and the parish to be served by two rectors of equal status, who preached on alternate weeks in the old church of St Nicholas and the new church of St Peter's (dedicated on 29 June 1704). The new church became the place of fashionable resort while the 'Old Church' of St Nicholas drew most of its congregation from amongst the 'lower orders'.

The growing population of Liverpool required additional church provision. In 1734, a new church, very much under Corporation patronage, designed by Thomas Steers, was built on the site of the former castle and dedicated to St George. During his sojourn in Liverpool, from 1750 until 1760, the former slaver captain, preacher and hymn writer, John Newton, author of 'Amazing Grace', worshipped in this church. As the century progressed other churches were built, notably St Thomas', consecrated in 1750 and famous for its 216 foot spire. St Paul's, built in 1769, had an impressive dome but appalling acoustics, and was later used for services in the Welsh language. Two private patrons paid for the erection of St Anne's church on the road to Everton in 1772. St James' church, in Parliament Street, was founded and built in 1775. In 1784 St John's church was built in the Old Haymarket. Between that date and the end of the century, a further four new Anglican churches were founded in the town. None of these new foundations had parochial status and each was, legally, a chapel of Liverpool Parish Church.

The old church of St Nicholas had a spire added to its ancient tower in 1746. The church underwent drastic modernisation in 1774 when the nave was pulled down and rebuilt in a Georgian 'Gothick' style. All this proved too much for the ancient steeple. On 11 February 1810 the spire and tower collapsed into the nave, killing over twenty people, the majority of whom were children from the Charity School. The tower was replaced by a new design of Thomas Harrison, completed in 1815, and it is the present tower of the church.

St Anne's church

The great expansion of population in the latter part of the eighteenth century placed extreme pressure on the ecclesiastical provision of Liverpool. Anxious that the opportunity for worship and instruction should be provided, both the Corporation and private individuals endowed churches. In this case it was the brothers Thomas and William Dodd, proprietors of the Richmond Woollen Hall, about which Moss is rather disparaging, who were the patrons when St Anne's was built in 1772. The brick church, uninspired in its design, has a notable place in the cultural development of Liverpool as it was the building where the Liverpool Choral Society performed the great oratorios of Handel and Haydn

PHOTO: LEN FENDER

Other denominations and faiths became established and are mentioned in Dr Moss' Guide Book. Three Presbyterian chapels were built, two Baptist meetings were created, a Quaker Meeting House, a Methodist chapel and a synagogue were to be found. The latter, founded prior to 1775, was one of the earliest Jewish communities in

England. Liverpool had always been something of a Protestant enclave in a largely Roman Catholic area of Lancashire. Roman Catholic worship was contrary to the law and practised in secret locations; not so secret that in 1745 the mob, in a fervour of anti-Jacobite enthusiasm, was able to sack and burn the Catholic chapel of St Mary in Edmond Street. It was not until the great Irish immigration

St Paul's church

One of the four churches sponsored by the Corporation, St Paul's, opened in 1769, in what was then Doghouse Lane, later known as St Paul's Square. The architect was Timothy Lightoller. Though of impressive appearance, with its dome and pediment, the church was unsuccessful because of its very poor acoustics. This fault was deemed unimportant when it was dedicated to services in the Welsh language. Miss M'Avoy, who lived in the square adjacent to the church in 1817, was reputed, though blind, to be able to recognise colours and to read print through touch. After briefly attracting fame, and some fortune, she was revealed as a fraud. The church was demolished in 1932.

of the nineteenth century that Liverpool became a major centre of Catholicism. The only Roman Catholic church that survives from this early period is that of St Peter's in Seel Street. Built in 1788, three years before the Catholic Relief Act, St Peter's is now the oldest surviving church building in the city centre, though no longer used for worship. Its inconspicuous architecture is a reminder that the later part of the eighteenth century could be a difficult time for Roman Catholics and that they were unwilling to draw attention to themselves.

In *Commutation-row*, on the left, is the *Blind Asylum*; where the blind poor are instructed in every mechanical art they are capable of attaining; which, while it assists in their support, makes them useful members of society. Their wares may be viewed and purchased on the spot. This charity is supported by voluntary contribution, is unconnected with the provision of the parish, and extends to objects from every part of the kingdom. – *See Blind Asylum*.

Passing the front of the Infirmary down *Shaw's Brow*; and turning to the left into the *Hay-market*, from whence will be seen *St John's Church*; we pass along *White-chapel* to the Hotel at bottom of Lord-street, where we commenced this latter part of our tour.

It will be perceived, that the street we last passed, with *Paradise-street* in the same continued direction, are nearly on a level, and lie low. It was in this direction, as mentioned in that the tide formerly flowed round this side of the town from the original pool where the Old Dock now is; which added considerably to its defence, and rendered it only accessible at the north end – hence its obstinate resistance to Prince Rupert. A walk through Paradise-street, which will afford a view of an elegant *dissenters chapel*, will best explain the course of the pool. At the other end of Paradise-street (formerly Common-shore) on the left, is *Hanover-street*; the more straight direction, is the bottom of *Duke-street*, formerly passed and the

The Fall of the Spire of St Nicholas Church

Early drawings show the church with a typical Lancashire square tower, sturdy and simple and with substantial corner buttresses. It was to enhance its usefulness as a navigational mark, that in 1746, a wooden spire was erected upon it. The additional weight on inadequate foundations soon raised fears for the security of the tower, especially when the bells rang. In 1789 a further £20 was spent on reinforcement. On February 11 1810, as the congregation gathered for the morning service, the north west corner of the tower collapsed and the spire fell into the nave, killing 22 people and injuring many more. The steeple was replaced by the present tower, designed by Thomas Harrison and completed in 1815. After recent refurbishment (2004–2005) the tower has been renamed the Landmark Tower and dedicated as a memorial to all Liverpool seafarers.

Junction of Fenwick Street and Brunswick Street,
pencil drawing by Matthew Gregson

The area adjacent to the Castle and between Castle Street and the waterfront
had been an area of small alleys, rope walks and open ground. Fenwick Street
or, as it was sometimes called 'Phoenix Street', was developed by the Moore
family in the second half of the seventeenth century and named after the family
of the wife of Sir Edward Moore. At one time, a part of the street was known
as 'Dry Bridge Street' after a foot bridge over the oldest rope walk in Liverpool.
Brunswick Street was opened in 1790 as a new development which cleared away
many of the smaller properties of the area.

turn on the right leads to the old Dock. The common sewer runs
under Paradise-street, White-chapel and even higher up, so that
in sudden and heavy rains, the inundation is such as to flood these
streets; and to fill the cellars, to the great terror and distress of their
inhabitants.

CHURCHES.

The town contains thirteen *churches of the established religion*; one of the *church of Scotland*; three *dissenters chapels*; a *quakers meeting*; four *methodists chapels*; two *baptist chapels*; three *Roman catholic chapels*; and a *Jewish synagogue*.

St. Nicholas, or the *Old Church* commonly so called from being first erected is of very ancient date; but there are no traces of its antiquity farther back than 1588; when it is recorded, that the Earl of Derby coming to his residence and waiting for a passage to the Isle of Man, the corporation erected and adorned a sumptuous stall in the church for his reception.* There formerly was a statue of St. Nicholas, in the church yard; to which the sailors presented offerings on their going to sea, to induce the saint to grant them a prosperous voyage.

This church was a parochial chapel under Walton, a neighbouring parish; till by act of Parliament, in 1699, Liverpool became a distinct parish. It contains some monuments of ancient and modern sculpture, but not interesting enough to engage the stranger's particular attention: a female figure, inclining over an urn, is most worthy his notice. Here are a peal of six bells, whose welcome notes announce the arrival of our ships from foreign voyages, chiefly the West Indies. Here is a good, but badly placed, organ. A spire was added to the tower, in 1750; and the walls of the church were rebuilt a few years ago. It is also intended to rebuild the pews and galleries. The church originally, was no doubt sufficiently sequestered; yet from the present, perhaps unavoidable, thoroughfares in every direction through the church yard, it but ill accords with the primitive intention of

> 'The church yard's lonely mound,
> Where melancholy with still silence reigns.'

---

* Seacombe's Memoirs.

St Peter's church

On the creation of the parish of Liverpool in 1699, with its highly unusual
provision of two rectors, it was decided that a new and worthy church was
needed in the more fashionable part of the town. The design of the building has
been ascribed to John Moffat. It was consecrated in 1704. Though the exterior
was undistinguished and rather bizarre, the interior was filled with lavishly
carved woodwork, in a style resembling that of Grinling Gibbons. It is thought
to have been carried out by local carvers who worked on the decoration of ships.
Portions of the carving, at the demolition of the church in 1922, were taken
to St Cuthbert's church, Churchtown, Southport and to the chapel in Banks,
Southport. The communion table from St Peter's is in daily use in Liverpool
parish church. The site of the church is commemorated by the name of Church
Street and the brass cross embedded in the pavement of that street.

A considerable portion of the lower part of this church is set apart for the public; and, as in most country churches, the men and women have different allotments. As these public seats are generally well filled, with very decent and orderly persons, devotion is better assisted than where the whole is a glare of dress and fashion: it induces a due sense of humility; and properly reminds us of the indistinction that is soon to take place in the state for which we are preparing.

St. Peter's was the next built church, and finished in 1704; which, with *St. Nicholas*, are the parish churches, over which two rectors preside. It is plain within; has a good organ; and a peal of eight bells, of good tone and well tuned. No sculpture or monuments worth a distinguished notice. – Regular oratorios, the first that were attempted in the north of England, were performed here in 1765, by performers, the principals of which were from London; who were not less surprised than gratified with the choruses, which were of this neighbourhood; the Lancashire chorus being still esteemed the best in the kingdom.

St. George's Church was consecrated in 1734. It will be found as elegant and well finished within as it is without. The altar, pulpit, organ loft, and the front of the galleries are, characteristically enough, of mahogany. It is the Mayor's chapel, where he attends every Sunday, and where are pews appropriated for *gentlemen*, including strangers, who choose to accompany him. A very good organ. No monumental inscriptions. The church is completely vaulted, for the purpose of a cemetery. On each side of the church is a terrace, with recesses underneath for the convenience of the market people. The octangular building, at each end of the church, on the south side, are offices for the clerk of the market and the nightly watch. In the recesses on each of the octangular parts of the steeple, is the painting of a saint: but so exposed a situation is very unfavourable to paintings.

St. Thomas's Church was consecrated in 1750; the whole of which, without and within, can no where, perhaps, be excelled in elegance and simplicity. In its very confined situation, it cannot be advantageously viewed in any direction. The south end of the

St John's church

The area of Shaw's Brow now William Brown Street, was, in the eighteenth
century, a random collection of buildings including the Infirmary and several
almshouses. In the period between 1775 and 1783 the church of St John was
erected to serve this community. The architect was probably Timothy Lightoller,
who had previously designed the domed church of St Paul's. At St John's he
adopted a new style producing a rather weak and undistinguished version of
Georgian Gothic. An important adjunct to the church was its burial ground
which relieved the pressure on the overcrowded cemeteries at St Peter's and St
Nicholas. It was at St John's that 240 French prisoners of war, who had died in
captivity, were buried. The church was demolished in 1899 and the site converted
into gardens where the good and the great are commemorated in sculpture.

church yard, and the bottom of Liver-street, afford the best views.
Its beautiful and lofty spire, however, has a pleasing effect from
every part of the town and the environs, where it can be seen. The
steeple and spire are 216 feet high; of which the spire forms the
greater part. A good Organ. No monuments.

St. Paul's Church was built at the public expence, and consecrated
in 1769. Its internal construction is so unfavourable to hearing,
notwithstanding the attempts that have been made to render it less
so, that it is but very thinly attended. The bottom of the church is
appropriated to the public. No Organ or monuments.

St. Ann's Church built in 1770 by two private proprietors, is a neat commodious church: has a painted window, and an organ: is remarkable for being placed in a north and south direction; and is viewed to advantage from the north road, and also from St. Ann-street. No monuments.

St. John's Church was finished at the public expence in 1784. It is plain within; and the lower part is laudably appropriated to the public. The church yard is also a public burial ground.

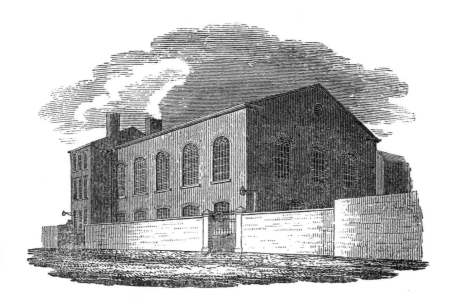

The Church of St Peter, Seel Street.

This church, built in 1788, was served by members of the Benedictine Order. Built before the Catholic Relief Act of 1791, it was deliberately designed to be inconspicuous, a simple brick box with a pedimented gable. There is little about the building, as depicted here, to draw attention to it or to give any indication of its denomination. Penal laws against the Catholic church were still on the statute books, though not enforced, and the community were not anxious to draw attention to themselves. The building, though it was extended and enlarged in 1817 and 1845, shows no signs of the triumphalism of Roman Catholic churches built after the repeal of the Laws in 1829, a trend superbly exemplified at St Francis Xavier (J. J. Scholes 1845) in Salisbury Street, Everton.

The Unitarian Chapel, Paradise Street

This handsome and strictly classical building reflects the wealth and social
importance of the congregation who worshipped in it. In the eighteenth century
there was a significant tendency amongst Presbyterian congregations to move to join
the Unitarian movement. The Unitarians were great proponents of humanitarian and
philanthropic causes. In Liverpool, prominent members of the congregation played
a significant part in the struggle to abolish the slave trade and later the institution
of slavery itself. Foremost amongst them were the Rathbone family, who were
associated with so many causes and generous benefactions.

Trinity Church can boast a peculiar neatness, externally and
internally; and is extremely commodious, the form and dimensions
being such as are well adapted to an auditory. An Organ; but
no monuments. It was consecrated in 1792; and built by private
proprietors.

St. James's Church not directly in the parish, was built about the
year 1774: is neat, commodious, and retired. An Organ; but no
monuments. Was built by private proprietors.

St. Catharine's, in Temple court; *St. Stephen's* in Byrom-street;
and *St. Mathew's* in Kay-street; formerly dissenting chapels; and
St. Mary's in Harrington-street; have nothing to recommend them

to the attention of the stranger, except neatness; but which surely must be a powerful recommendation to a congregation.

The *Scotch church*, or *kirk*, at the top of Renshaw-street; the three *dissenters chapels* in Benn's Garden, Renshaw-street and Paradise-street; the *Quaker's Meeting* in Hunter-street; the four *Methodist chapels* in Pitt-street, Mount-pleasant, Edmund-street, and Maguire-street; the two *Baptist chapels* in Stanley-street and Byrom-street; the three *Roman Catholic chapels* in Lumber-street, Seel-street and Sir Thomas's Buildings; and the *Jew's Synagogue* in Pitt-street; are all fitted up in a manner becoming their several relative customs. The Paradise-street Dissenting chapel is the only

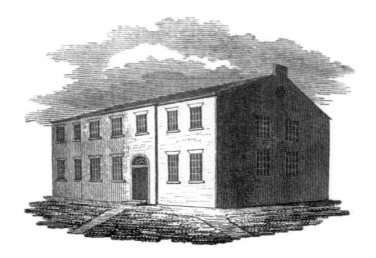

The Quaker Meeting House

The Society of Friends tended to draw its early members from amongst the skilled artisans and mercantile classes. It gained an early membership in Liverpool and the first meeting house was established in Hackin's Hey, where Quaker Alley still remains. At the time when Moss was writing, the Meeting House with its graveyard was abandoned and they moved to these new premises in Hunter Street. Some of the most important philanthropists in early-nineteenth-century Liverpool belonged to the Society of Friends and they were also heavily involved in the commercial development of the town.

PHOTO: LEN FENDER.

one that claims particular regard as a public edifice. It is a beautiful structure; but so situated, that in no direction can it be viewed to advantage; nor is it sufficiently retired for devotion – disadvantages that surely might have been avoided in a new erection. That elegant simplicity – *simplex munditiis* – noticed in some of the before-mentioned churches, is not so well preserved here, *within*. The inlaid work round the galleries, in the manner of cabinet work, and the airy flight of steps to the still more airy pulpit, have a tawdriness and levity not the best adapted to a place of serious devotion. The pews are very conveniently disposed. The organ is very neat; and is a rare instance of that instrument in that situation. Behind the chapel, is a charity school, supported chiefly, and much to their honour, by the frequenters of the chapel.

Many of the churches have clocks; none of which has a bell sufficiently large to be heard at a distance. It would be much to the credit and benefit of the town, to have one something like St. Paul's in London, as a *general monitor*. The advantages are too obvious to need enumerating.

The Town Hall

Few towns or cities have a civic building of the elegance and architectural merit of Liverpool. However, the history of the Town Hall is complex and little is known of the earliest period. It is probable that in the early days of the borough the house of the Mayor provided the meeting place for the Corporation, while the chapel of St Nicholas could be used for the town assemblies, held annually on St Luke's Day (October 18), for the election of the Mayor. In 1515, John Crosse, bequeathed to the town a common hall which stood at the junction of Castle Street, Water Street and Dale Street. It was known as St Mary's Hall but after the Reformation became known by its secular title of Exchange or Common Hall. There the Mayor's court met and it also served as the town's lock-up and custom's warehouse. Almost nothing is known about this building, except that its thatched roof was replaced in 1567.

As Liverpool's great expansion began the old hall was deemed too small and unworthy and a new Exchange was planned for the boom town. In 1673 Richard Blome in his 'Magna Britannia' wrote 'Here is now erecting at the publick charge of the Mayor, aldermen, etc.; a famous town house, placed upon pillars and arches of hewn stone, and underneath is the publick Exchange for merchants'. The building was completed the following year and admired by Celia Fiennes as '… a very pretty Exchange stands on eight pillars beside the corners which are each pillars all of stone … over which is a very handsome Town Hall – over all is a tower and cupilow'. This building served for nearly seventy years as the civic centre of the town.

In 1748 Sarah Clayton, the leading business woman of Liverpool, vetted the suitability of John Wood of Bath as the architect for a projected new hall. A new site, immediately adjacent to the old Exchange, was purchased and cleared. The foundation stone was laid on 14 September 1749 and the hall completed by 1754. The new Exchange was built in the Corinthian style with the lower floor still envisaged as a place of business with a central courtyard and arches to the street. This arrangement was soon abandoned and the courtyard was enclosed. On each of the two visible fronts – those on the south and east – there were pediments and pilasters interspersed with carvings, mainly representative of the African trade. The whole was surmounted by an ugly square cupola topped by a stone lantern. This feature seems unlikely to have been a part of Wood's original design but may have been added at the request of the Corporation. During the riots of unemployed sailors in 1775, the Exchange was one of the targets of their attacks with muskets and canon dragged from the ships. The building was stalwartly defended by men recruited by the Mayor and suffered superficial damage. The damage would have been worse had not the sporting instincts of the rioters led them to target the large carving of the Liver Bird on the pediment or, as they put it, 'Shoot the goose', rather than to cannonade the lower floors.

In the early 1780s plans for improvements were made. The cupola was removed in 1786. In 1788 John Foster, who held an unofficial position as the Corporation's architect, designed further improvements but he was ordered to consult with James Wyatt. Over the next few years an extensive modification programme was put in hand, including new facades on the north and west faces. The new Town Hall was to be topped by an elegant central dome, surmounted by a figure of Minerva. On 18 January 1795 the whole of the Exchange building was gutted by fire and one life was lost. The decision was made to rebuild within the

The Exchange, 1770

This engraving by the distinguished topographical artist, engraver and cartographer Peter Burdett, shows the Town Hall or the Exchange, as it was more usually called at that period, as it was designed by John Woods of Bath. In the original plan the heavily rusticated ground floor with its round headed arches was to remain open to provide a trading place, as the pillared basement of the old Exchange had been. However, it proved too dark and congested and the trading floor was transferred to an open space behind the building. To provide additional accommodation the arches were glazed and the ground floor subdivided.

existing outer walls which were little damaged. The work was entrusted to Wyatt as the supervisor and Foster as the local architect and interior designer. Subsequently, various extensions and modifications have been made to both the interior and exterior of the building. Today the elegant and lavish interior of the Town Hall displays Foster's skill and the early nineteenth century wealth and civic pride of Liverpool.

THE EXCHANGE.

The inside of this handsome edifice, (except the new north end) was entirely destroyed by accidental fire, on the 18th January, 1795. The lower part was originally formed like the Royal Exchange, in London, and designed for the like purpose. Over the walks, were the *Borough Court-room*, the Mayor's office, the *Council Chamber*, and the *Assembly Rooms*; all of which, with their valuable furniture, were consumed.

The whole of the original Exchange was appropriated to a *ball* and *supper*, given to the principal inhabitants by the corporation,

View of the Town Hall or Exchange

The viewpoint of this drawing is on the Exchange Flags. The left hand facade of the Town Hall on High Street is the original design of John Wood (1754). The rear elevation is part of the extension and refurbishment carried out by Wyatt and John Foster after the fire of 1795. It is in this portion of the building that some of the most sumptuous rooms are to be found, notably the dinning room and the great ballroom. In this view the spire St George's church is visible in the background.

on his Majesty's recovery, in April, 1789. All the lower area was formed into a supper room; superbly illuminated with pillars and festoons of lamps, in the central parts; the walls enlivened by transparent emblematic painting; and *eight hundred* well dressed persons, of both sexes, sat commodiously down together to as elegant a supper as art could devise and taste display. A more splendid and uncommon spectacle, than that exhibited, cannot well be conceived: the effect was wonderful. A *stranger* present, pleasantly and neatly enough, observed; that the whole, though uncommonly splendid, became more particularly enchanting under the fascinating influence of five hundred *Lancashire witches*.

The Exchange in future will be converted into coffee-rooms and offices for the convenience of the merchant, and for transacting the public business of the town. All the upper part of the new or north side, is to form an *Assembly-room*; and a cupola will be placed upon the centre. The front of the new part appears, at a little distance, as if unfinished, by the exposure of the high projecting roof. The four statuary figures are emblematic of the four quarters of the world; and the fronts of the new part are said to display great architectural taste.

The pediment of the south front contains a piece of highly finished sculpture in bold *relief.* The small figures in the left angle, represent the *infant commerce* of the town; one of which seems watching over the different articles of merchandise, and another embraces the *liver* with the right arm, under the auspices of *liberty*, with the *cap* in one hand, the other being supported by the *fasces*; denoting *liberty* under the direction of the *civil power.* The large *projecting figure*, with a defending sword in the right hand over a shield bearing the *liver*, and a *cornucopia*; is the *Genius of commerce*, protecting the *infant commerce* of the town with one hand, and directing the attention of *Neptune*, for the same intention, with the other. The hoary *god of the ocean*, with the *trident* resting on the right arm, reclining with the left on a *watery urn*, is a bold figure; the attention in the adverted countenance, is well and greatly expressed. Part of the *hull*, *masts* and *flag* of a *ship*, fill up the right angle. This emblematic prediction has, hitherto, been happily accomplished.

The first stone of the Exchange was laid in September, 1749; and the two original fronts, independent of some grotesque ornaments then in fashion, which the chisel would improve, are considered to form a chaste and well-executed piece of architecture. The whole, when properly insulated and finished, will, no doubt, have a good effect in every direction. The

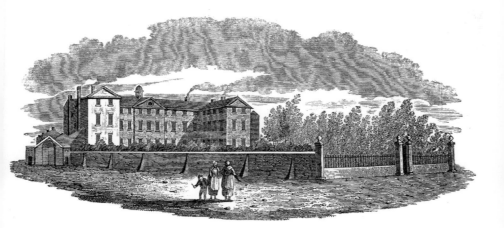

The Workhouse

After the Poor Law Amendment Act of 1834, workhouses were often referred to as 'Bastilles' because they were perceived as places of confinement and punishment for poverty. This was not the original intention when they were visualised as places where the poor could be served in two ways. Firstly, they would be employed – usually in manual tasks – but on a commercial basis. The profits which might accrue could be offset against the costs of the maintenance of the building and the support of the inmates. Secondly, it was thought that by training the paupers to carry our tasks they might be taught a trade and become capable of earning their own living. Problems arose when local tradesmen found their work undercut by the products of the workhouse. It was also difficult to find useful tasks for an unskilled labour force who lacked any inducement to work. The adjacent house of correction was intended to administer a salutary lesson to minor criminals and malefactors.

principal entrance will be from the south front, which will open into a vestibule leading to a grand spiral staircase of stone, lighted from a dome, that will communicate with the upper parts of the building.

THE POOR HOUSE.

Remarkable for the boldness of its structure, airy situation, and the space it occupies. It was furnished in 1771, at an expence of 8,000l. and has since received considerable additions. It will contain about 1500 persons. – The *House of Correction* adjoins the Poor House.

ALMS HOUSES.

These asylums of poverty and old age, were formerly distributed in different parts of the town. Becoming in a state of decay, they were all pulled down, and very commodious ones erected in their stead in an open space behind the Poor House; where the poor inhabitants have the benefit of pure air.

THE INFIRMARY.

This public charity was opened in 1749. It was built and is supported, as most provincial hospitals are, by public contributions. It contains about 200 beds, and admits patients from all quarters. It relieves out-patients. The situation is airy, extended and commodious.

LUNATIC HOSPITAL.

This is behind, and contiguous to, the Infirmary. It is to be regretted that this, like other similar institutions, is not a *complete charity*, to admit patients free of expence. This perhaps will no where be fully obtained till an asylum is constructed upon a more extended plan, fixed in a central part of a country, and made an open general concern. As it is, the affluent are conducted to private asylums; the parish poor are sent hither at the parish expence; whilst many of the middle rank are deprived of proper assistance, in the most dreadful malady human nature can suffer under, from an inability to purchase it. The objects of these, so necessary, institutions, have not, surely, been properly considered.

Insanity is a growing malady, no doubt arising from the increasing dissipations and excesses of the age.

The Blue Coat School or Hospital

The Bluecoat Chambers is the oldest building in central Liverpool. It was in 1708 that one of the rectors of Liverpool, the Rev. Robert Styth and a wealthy merchant and sea-captain Bryan Blundell became concerned about the plight of the numerous orphans who thronged the town. They set up a day school, then known as a hospital, in a building near the church of St Peter. It was intended to house fifty boys, though later girls were accepted. It was funded by subscription to which Blundell contributed substantially from his own pocket. A master was to be employed at an annual salary of £20. Funding proved inadequate and Bryan Blundell sustained the school mainly from his resources, contributing a further £250 over a five year period up to 1713. It was laid down in the foundation documents that the children were to be housed, clothed and fed and taught 'to read, write and cast accounts' while girls were also instructed in 'knitting and housewifery'. As the Latin inscription on the facade of the building tells us all were to be taught 'according to the principles of the Church of England'. The age of admission was nine years and they were put out as apprentices at the age of fourteen. Moss relates how the school supplemented its income by employing the children in the making of pins.

In 1713 Robert Styth died and for much of the time Blundell was at sea. In the absence of its two principal benefactors the school went into a decline and the children of the school were to be seen begging on the streets. Blundell resolved to give up the sea and to remain ashore, trading as a merchant and devoting much of his income to charitable causes. In order to renew the school he launched another subscription which raised the great total of £3,000, to which Blundell personally contributed £750.

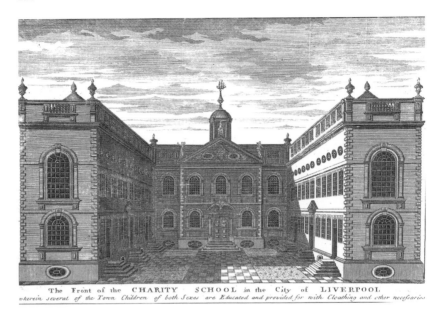

The Front of the CHARITY SCHOOL in the City of LIVERPOOL
wherein several of the Town Children of both Sexes are Educated and provided for with Cleathing and other necessaries

The Blue Coat Charity School

Dating from 1718 the Blue Coat Chambers is now the oldest building in central Liverpool. The original architect is unknown but both Thomas Ripley and Thomas Steers are possible designers. Built in a soft, red brick with white painted window and door cases, the lintels of the windows decorated with cherubs heads, it it still clearly recognisable as the building shown here. Severely damaged and restored in the Second World War the present building has lost some of its exuberance. In this engraving the cupola has a wind vane in the shape of a ship, reminiscent of the one still to be found on the parish church.

A new, larger plot of land, close to the original school was given by the Corporation and the newly designed building arose. The architect of the school is unknown but both Thomas Ripley, who had designed the Custom House at the Dock, and Thomas Steers have been suggested. It is a handsome and restrained building of red brick with painted stone dressings around the doors – one of which has a pediment – windows and corner quoins. The building opened in 1718 and in 1721 the former charity school was leased by the Corporation to house the town's free grammar school which until that time. occupied the old chapel of St Mary, adjacent to St Nicholas Church.

Shortly after this (c. 1723) space at the rear of the building was used to build a quadrangle surrounded by thirty six almshouses.

Bryan Blundell proved to be a very successful merchant and became established in the elite of the town, serving as Mayor on two occasions. Much of his fortune was spent on charitable enterprises and it was calculated that he had given a total of £3,000 to philanthropic use. For many years he served as Treasurer to the Trustees of the School.

Over the years the building was much altered internally and externally though the facade facing Church Alley remained largely untouched until the school moved in 1906 into their new building at Wavertree. The old building was purchased from the Trustees by Lord Leverhulme and presented to the city. During the Second World War the building sustained severe damage. Restoration was undertaken immediately after the war. The reconstructed building had a new severity of appearance with the removal of some of the more extravagant decorative features. The renovated building was opened to coincide with the Festival of Britain in 1951 and renamed the Bluecoat Chambers. The Chambers housed offices, shops, exhibition areas, craft workshops and artist's studios. During 2005–7 a further major renovation and modernisation has taken place.

THE DISPENSARY.

This neat edifice is situated in Church-street, a little above the church. As it is very accessible to the sick poor, great numbers have been daily assisted by it since its institution in 1778. It is supported by voluntary contributions and annual subscriptions, the latter of which amount to about 500l.

SEAMEN'S HOSPITAL.

This charity, adjoining the Infirmary, was instituted in 1752, for the maintenance of decayed seamen, their widows and children; and is supported by sixpence a month out of the wages of every seaman sailing out of the port.

BLUE COAT HOSPITAL.

This structure (in School-lane, behind St. Peter's Church) was raised so long ago as the year 1720. It contains 79 orphan children, 143 fatherless children, and 58 whose parents are in indigent circumstances; being in the whole 280; of which 230 are boys, and 50 girls: they are all cloathed, fed and lodged: the boys are taught reading, writing and accounts; and those intended for the sea are instructed in navigation; the girls are taught reading, writing, spinning, sewing, knitting and housewifery: they are all at school one half of the day, and work the other half: many of the boys are employed in making pins; they are admitted at eight, and put out apprentices at fourteen years old. It is supported by benefactions, legacies, &c. and annual subscriptions, at an expence exceeding 1200l. a year.

This Hospital, and the Infirmary and Dispensary, are assisted by charity sermons at all the churches, and by an annual play at the theatre.

Charitable Institutions of Liverpool

The charitable instinct was not a creation of the eighteenth century but during that period it underwent a change in its organisation, motivation and implementation. In the Middle Ages, charitable giving had relied on either the benevolence of the Church or on private benefactions in providing relief to the poor, the needy, and the sick. The endowment of charities was made in the hope of earning remission of sins and creating a memorial to the donor. In post Reformation England this social network was virtually destroyed but the problems of the poor, the unemployed and the marginalised persisted. During the Tudor period, motivated by Christian charity and concern for the potential for unrest and disorderly behaviour, new obligations on local, parochial government were created to try to deal with the situation. These culminated in the Elizabethan Poor Law of 1601, which created two categories of the poor, the 'Deserving Poor' those, who through no fault of their own, needed support and the 'Sturdy Rogues and Vagabonds', who, it was considered, had chosen an irresponsible and idle life. After various modifications, this Act provided a social support system throughout the seventeenth and eighteenth centuries, indeed parts of the legislation remained in force until 1947.

However, in the time when Dr Moss was writing, a change in attitude is perceptible. He describes a number of Liverpool institutions which were organised as private initiatives to deal with a perceived special need in the community, undertaking various aspects of care for the indigent or the sick, whether sick sailors, the insane or unmarried, pregnant women.

There were a number of motives for this change in public awareness of poverty and distress. The old Poor Law had been based on a rural economy and society which was swiftly passing away. Its parochial organisation ensured that the various categories of the poor and disabled were only present in small numbers. In many cases they had familial support, and they were well known and possibly even viewed with affection in their communities. The evidence is that, at

The North Front of the Sailors Hospital.

The Sailors' Hospital

Located on Shaw's Brow adjacent to the Infirmary this refuge for 'decayed sailors, their widows and children' was originally proposed in 1747 but it was not until 1752 that the buildings were erected and the management structures set up. In the foreground is Townsend Mill while in the distance both St George's and St Peter's churches can be discerned.

this time, the Poor Law was very often humane and generous, far from being the brutal and harsh system of the workhouse that it became in the nineteenth century.

The social conditions in the ever-growing urban centres were very different. The needy were often strangers and thronged the towns in such numbers that the mechanisms of the Poor Law were increasingly stretched. The urban middle class had only to walk the streets to be confronted with those in need of help. This confrontation could either stimulate revulsion and hostility or arouse an instinct to 'do something'. It may be that this instinct was encouraged by the religious climate of the period. The eighteenth century saw the emergence of the evangelical tradition which was particularly strong amongst the urban, mercantile and commercial middle class. The Unitarian Church was especially influential and heavily emphasised the need to care for humanity. The members of this denomination were represented in most of the humanitarian and philanthropic movements of the period. The development of the evangelical Anglican tradition and the emergence of Methodism gave added impetus to the provision of social relief, provided the recipients were duly submissive and grateful.

Laudable as this was, there was probably another instinct at work. The new urban structures lacked a social leadership. An aristocracy of wealth and influence was emerging but there was a great deal of competition and often a steely determination to ascend the greasy pole of Liverpool society. To work for a charity, to sit on the committee was a badge of success and recognition. A glance at the list of organisers and committee members of the various Liverpool institutions shows that the people involved were drawn from a narrow social band and were often involved in a number of civic charitable activities.

BLIND ASYLUM.

This charity was established in 1790, and is supported at an annual expence of about 300l. It is proposed to erect a compact building for the better convenience of the several manufactures, &c. The Charity finds materials, and the poor are paid for their labour in the manufactory, under the direction of their teachers. Most of these unfortunate objects have lost their sight by the small-pox. It is to be lamented that so great a majority of the poor still retain their

School for the Blind

Credit for the establishment of this institution was claimed by various local people and, in truth, perhaps it was a synthesis of various contributions, though Matthew Gregson had a major role in rousing interest and providing funds. The School first opened in 1791 in two adjacent buildings on Commutation Row, so-called because the houses were designed to avoid the window tax. In 1800 the demand had outstripped the premises and the School moved to London Road. This is the building shown in this engraving, the lower illustration shows projected extensions. A further move was needed in 1851 when the School was established in Hardman Street.

prejudices against inoculation. A plan of a general inoculation was formed here some years ago, and every persuasive means made use of to induce the lower ranks to accept it; but to so little effect at last, that after a trial of two or three years, it was given up.*

The men are here employed in making lobby-cloths and bears; baskets of different kinds; whips; and clock and window cords. The women spin the yarn for the window cords, and for sail cloth and linen cloth; they make mops; and some are taught music, both instrumental and vocal. One of the girls is possessed of a voice rarely equalled.

SUNDAY SCHOOLS.

These pleasing institutions have long been established here, and are very numerous. The children are instructed in schools appropriate to the purpose, and attend the service of the different churches every Sunday, twice. The early impression of divine and moral duties upon the minds of a class of our fellow creatures who might otherwise remain uninformed of them, must produce effect so salutary and extensive, as not to be very readily calculated; and which prove highly grateful on reflection.

INSTITUTION FOR RESTORING DROWNED PERSONS.

Drowning is an accident so frequent here, as to render this institution very necessary. Above 400 persons have become objects of it since its institution, in 1775, more than one half of whom have been restored. A guinea is given to those who take up a body, if it be afterward restored to life; if not restored, half a

---

* Innoculation, the Turkish practice of introducing a weakened strain of smallpox into children to create immunity, was introduced into England by Lady Mary Wortley-Montague in the early decades of the eighteenth century. Though effective, it was a difficault and possibly dangerous procedure. It was superseded by the use of vaccination which made used of the related but more benign Cowpox and was pioneered by Edward Jenner (D.B,, 2007).

Directions for Restoring to Life Persons apparently drowned.

The greatest exertions should be used to take out the body before one hour elapses, and the Process immediately employed.

Not to be held up by the heels ; nor rolled on casks, or other rough usage ; avoid the use of Salt, in all cases of apparent death.

1.—Convey carefully the body, with the head raised, to the nearest convenient public house.

2.—Strip, and dry the body :— clean the mouth and nostrils.

3.—Young Children:—put between two persons in a warm bed.

4.—Adults: —lay the body on a blanket or bed, and in cold weather near the fire. In the warm season air should be freely admitted.

5.—To be gently rubbed with flannel sprinkled with spirits, and a heated warm pan, covered, lightly moved over the back and spine.

6.—To restore breathing.—Introduce the pipe of a pair of bellows (when no apparatus) into *one* nostril ; close the mouth and

* K

Instructions for Restoring Drowned Persons

As can be imagined there was a considerable danger of drowning in eighteenth century Liverpool with its urban waterfront and unfenced docks in the centre of the town. Dr Thomas Houlson of the Infirmary, had encountered an institution for the recovery of the drowned while studying at the University of Leiden. In 1775 he suggested the establishment of a similar organisation to tackle the problem. A reception house was erected on the docks and rewards were given to those who recovered victims who were successfully treated. Instructions on treatment were circulated to the public. Initially, the organisation had a 72% success rate, though some of the recommended methods using tobacco smoke blown into the rectum seem bizarre today. In 1822 the responsibility for rescue and treatment of the drowned was undertaken by the Corporation.

guinea. It is at the Corporation's expence. Long poles with hooks at the ends, are dispersed in different places about the docks, for the purpose of dragging for those persons who fall in.

BENEVOLENT SOCIETY.

The intention of this society is to seek for poor obscure objects who, from diffidence, Infirmity, or as strangers, cannot obtrude themselves so as to make their wants known; and for this intention, the members alternately visit every obscure recess of poverty and wretchedness they can discover, to relieve the present urgent

The Theatre Royal Williamson Square, drawing by James Brierley

The Theatre Royal was financed by a share issue of £6000 in thirty shares and was built to a design based on one of Sir William Chambers. The Theatre opened in June 1772 with a Prologue written by George Coleman and spoken by Mr Younger, one of the managers, before the audience enjoyed the tragedy of 'Mahomet' and the farce 'The Deuce is in him'. The theatre was played by some of the most distinguished actors and actresses of the day, who, as Moss tells us, were not always well-received by the Liverpool audience. In 1798, the leading actor John Palmer dropped dead on the stage after speaking the words 'there is another and a better world'. In its final days the building was used as a cold-storage depot.

PHOTO: LEN FENDER.

necessities of their suffering inmates, till more effectual assistance can be procured. This society may be justly styled *benevolent*.

THE LADIES CHARITY.

This *last*, although not *least valuable*, of the public charities which adorn the town, was long in contemplation, but was only effected in 1796. Its intention is the relief of poor married women, in childbed, at their own homes; a mode that proves to have many advantages over a public hospital. Proper assistants, male and female, are appointed; as also a *matron*, to provide every necessary of food, &c. that may be wanted; by which means the poor and their offspring are rescued from the injuries arising from improper treatment, and are restored and preserved, with comfort to themselves, to that society from which many, in this trying situation, have been severed by ignorance and want. The charity is very properly under the patronage of *ladies*, with a *lady patroness* at their head; and the accounts necessarily conducted by a *committee of gentlemen*. It is supported by annual subscription, and by other gratuitous benefactions and contributions; and its various comforts have already been sensibly felt.

THE THEATRE.

The present house was opened in 1772. It is sufficiently spacious and commodious. Liverpool formerly boasted the first set of performers out of London. The house was only open in the summer months and when the London theatres were shut, and the best of the performers were selected for the season. Of late, however, from the increase of theatrical rage, the number of provincial theatres have so much increased, as to divide the London performers; nay, they are mostly turned *strollers*; exhibiting themselves for a few nights, separately, in all parts of the united dominions. Formerly no performer, of whatever rank, could be admitted to perform here without being engaged for the whole of the season; during which regulation, the performances were supported by a regular succession of the first performers of the London stages. The house still regularly opens about the close of the London houses, and shuts at their re-opening.

The town made a successful resistance to the first introduction of provincial performers in the summer season, of whom *Mrs. Siddons* and *Mr. John Kemble* formed a part. The latter was hissed off the stage; and *Mrs. Siddons*, who had played here in former winter seasons, and was favourably received in both the walks of tragedy and comedy, was, fortunately for herself as it has since turned out, compelled to quit the town. So versatile is public opinion, that on her first reappearing here after having received the stamp of approbation from a London audience, they who had

been so desirous to banish her the theatre, were now so eager
to see her perform, that many injuries, both of body and dress,
were sustained, so great was the pressures of the crowd to get
admittance into the play-house Since that time, the group has
become more motley – *'a thing of shreds and patches.'* Mrs. Mattocks
has played here, with little interruption, in the summer season,
for thirty years, with deserving estimation. A benefit play is given
every season for the public charities.

Liverpool's Cultural Revolution

Writing in 1795, James Wallace in his 'General & Descriptive History'
wrote 'Arts and sciences are inimical to the spot [Liverpool],
absorbed in the nautical vortex, the only pursuit of the inhabitants
is COMMERCE'. The Liverpool merchant of the first part of the
eighteenth century has been characterised as 'a mercantilist, materialist
and an empiricist whose pleasures were to be found in conspicuous
consumption and consumerism'. When they met for social purposes it
was in the convivial atmosphere of The Ugly Face Club, 1743, or the
Mock Corporation of Sefton which met from 1753 until 1829 and had
no purpose but sociability.

When William Moss was writing a marked change in the cultural
life of the town was taking place and his work is a component
in a search for a new identity by the prosperous middle class of
Merseyside. In part, this was a response to a growing criticism of the
town which was being made as an element of the slavery abolition
campaign. From the foundation of the Abolition Society in 1787 the
town, its participation in the African Trade and the cultural and
moral probity of its inhabitants came under ferocious attack. This
had two effects. The merchants, far from restricting their traffic, plied
it even more vigorously, while the influential inhabitants tried to create
a new image of Liverpool, and themselves, as cultured, civilised and
urbane.

By c. 1750 there were already some indicators of social change. A
theatre had been built and proved successful. In 1758 the first English
subscription library was founded in Liverpool. In the 1770s attempts
were made to inaugurate a literary and philosophical society and an

academy of art but met with very limited success. In 1786 a concert hall was built in Bold Street. The performances there supplemented the existing tradition of oratorios, sacred music and other choral events in various locations. To enhance education, visiting lecturers provided courses, mainly on subjects drawn from natural philosophy.

In the 1790s William Roscoe became the paradigm for the new-style Liverpool gentleman. His scholarship, breadth of outlook, radical and abolitionist credentials were seen as contradicting the portrayal of the Liverpool man of the day. His work on renaissance Florence led to comparisons with Liverpool and the mercantile elite were happy to

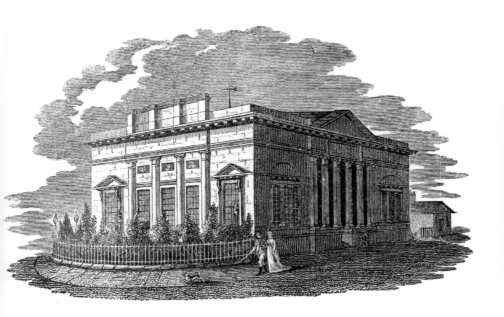

The Lyceum, Bold Street

Among the first of the new academic and social institutions of eighteenth century Liverpool was the Liverpool Library, the first in Britain (1758). This developed, in 1800, into a new body known as the Lyceum. Its members acquired a site at the foot of Bold Street and commissioned Thomas Harrison to build their new premises, in a chaste, neoclassical design. The gentlemen's club closed in the late twentieth century and the building has since served as a cafe, a post office and is now (2007) a bar.

assume the role of Lorenzo the Magnificent, men of business but also cultured, artistic, educated, patrons of the arts and sciences.

With Roscoe setting the pace, the developments came thick and fast and these new institutions, now in the spirit of their times, were to prove much more durable than their predecessors. In 1797 the Athenaeum with its newsroom for the commercial man and its scholar's library was founded and epitomised the new duality of interests. Its success inspired the Liverpool Library to revitalise itself as the Lyceum, in a new building at the foot of Bold Street. The controversy aroused by this led to a faction amongst the members forming the Union Newsroom in Duke Street. A feature of these organisations was the way in which a deliberate attempt was made to bring together men – they were exclusively male preserves – from the various aspects of the commercial, political and religious life of the town in peaceful harmony. The new cultural tendency was set and during the early decades of the nineteenth century Liverpool was foremost in Britain in the foundation of cultural and educational societies. In 1812 a new Literary and Philosophical Society was inaugurated. Its members played a major part in a variety of initiatives from petitioning for the release of corpses for medical dissection to cultivating the popularity of Gothic architecture. Many of these societies came together in 1814 in the Royal Institution, fufilling Roscoe's dream of a central cultural organisation, in which men of all persuasions and interests could come together for the pleasures of intellectual fulfillment.

PUBLIC CONCERTS.

The *Public Concert Room* is in Bold-street.* It is large, and finished with great elegance. The seat below and in the gallery are well disposed for a number of auditors; yet the amphitheatre form is, no doubt, better adapted to a concert-room; not only for hearing the music, but for viewing the company. It seems the present form, of a large secluded gallery, was adopted to gain room for the accommodation of the *musical festival*, which was

---

* This is esteemed a good street and neighbourhood.

intended to take place once in three years. It will admit 1300 persons, commodiously. The *orchestra* is well formed and arranged. The *organ* is more powerful than fine toned, and has a great effect in choruses and full pieces. Some gentlemen perform in the instrumental parts on public nights; but the *principals* are all supported by professional men of merit, who take frequent opportunities of displaying their several abilities in solos, duos. &c. the vocal department is no less ably filled by professional performers: so that the concerts, which are miscellaneous, would go well off, if the vocal accompanyments of what should be only the auditory, would be *tacet*, or even *piano*.

The concerts are supported by annual subscriptions of two guineas each; which admit three persons to each performance, by tickets in the name of a gentleman subscribers; which are transferable to ladies, and to the younger sons of subscribers; but a resident gentleman cannot be admitted unless by tickets at 3s. 6d. each. A lady who is a stranger will be admitted by the ticket of a subscriber. The number of annual concerts, is twelve; and the subscribers, about 300. Here is also a distinct subscription to a *Choral Concert*, where selections from the *oratorios*, &c. are performed.

ASSEMBLIES.

The *Assembly-room* in the Exchange having been burnt down, a temporary one is substituted in the Hotel at the bottom of Lord-street; till the new one, in the former place, is completed. The assemblies are in the winter season; they commence in October, and terminate on the King's birth-day. They are supported by subscription; and strangers are admitted by tickets. They are generally pretty well attended. A lady and gentleman preside, as is usual on these occasions, over the decorum of the room.

LONDON TAVERN and TALBOT INN, WATER-STREET,

THE   ROYAL

MAIL   COACH,

With a GUARD   All the WAY,

SETS out from the above INN, every NIGHT, at NINE O'CLOCK, and goes in THIRTY HOURS, to the SWAN WITH TWO NECKS, in LAD-LANE, LONDON.

The public are respectfully informed, that a POST COACH, with four insides only, began on the 4th June, 1792, and sets off every evening, at five o'clock; arrives in London the morning of the second day, at five o'clock, being only thirty-six hours.

Also, the BIRMINGHAM and OXFORD COACH, every morning, at ten o'clock, Sunday excepted.

Likewise, the BATH and BRISTOL COACH.

LIVERPOOL and YORK MAIL COACH, in ONE DAY.

N. B. The Proprietors of the above Coaches will not be accountable for any parcel that is above the value of 5l. unless entered as such, and an adequate premium paid for the same, viz. 3d. for each pound value, as insurance, over and above the common carriage by weight.

'and to receive the same, on which payment the interest on such in-
stalments will cease.

MARTIN PETRIE, Sec.

For PHILADELPHIA,
The American Ship **ATLANTIC,**
SILAS SWAIN, Master,
To sail about the 10th of August.
Burthen 350 tons; well known to have the very best
accommodations for passengers. For freight or passage apply to
George Green, Broker, or to ROBERT BENT.

To sail in a few days,
For NEW YORK,
The American Ship **ALEXANDER,**
ALEX COFFIN, Master,
(A Constant Trader)
Burthen 280 tons, has good accommodations for passengers. For
freight or passage apply to the Captain on board, in King's Dock,
George Green, Broker, or to ROBERT BENT.

MONDAY's MAIL.

Liverpool Advertiser 8 August 1793

The first newspaper published in Liverpool was *Williamson's Advertiser*, which
appeared on 28 May 1756. Billinge's paper was a rival and competitor until the
papers were merged. The papers of this period were mainly concerned with
local commercial and shipping information and national news was very much
a secondary preoccupation. The pages illustrated show these concerns and are
especially interesting, in the notices carried of coach services from Liverpool
and its representations of contemporary ships.

CHEAP TRAVELLING
THROUGH BIRMINGHAM TO LONDON.

BY the TRAVELLER, post-coach, from the Fleece Inn,
Dale-street, Liverpool, every Monday, Wednesday and
Friday afternoons, at four o'clock, through Northwich,
Middlewich, Newcastle, Stone, and Stafford; dines at Birmingham, and arrives in London very early the next morning. Inside fare to Birmingham 1l. 5s. outside 14s.; inside
to London 2l. 10s. outside 1l. 8s. Small parcels to Birmingham 1s. each, and 1d. per lb.; Ditto to London 2s. each, and
2d per lb. Performed by J. DUNN and Co.
N. B. The proprietors cannot be accountable for any parcel or passengers' luggage above 5l. value, unless entered and
paid for accordingly.

COFFEE HOUSES.

The *Coffee-room* in the Hotel, at the bottom of Lord-street, is neat and roomy; and is supplied with most of the London and provincial *newspapers*; and with *magazines, reviews, army* and *navy lists*, &c. There is a book in which is entered the name, cargo, and place sailed from, of every vessel that arrives in the port. It has a list of between three and four hundred annual subscribers, at a guinea each. Strangers have the free privilege of the room; which is often crowded; in an evening particularly. Notwithstanding its airy appearance, the room is very close, often offensively so; seemingly for want of attention to ventilation. Coffee, &c. are supplied within the adjoining tavern.

The *Coffee-room* in Exchange Alley, on the west side of the Exchange, is very neat, airy and comfortable; and as the subscribers are not so numerous as at the Hotel, it is more retired than the latter. The accommodation of *newspapers*, &c. are nearly the same as at the Hotel; as also the admission of strangers. A waiter attends to supply *coffee*, &c.

The *Merchants Coffee house* in the Old Church yard, is much smaller than the others; and its accommodations are proportionate. Commanding a view of the river and signal poles, it is conveniently situated for attending to the movements of the shipping.

There is a *tennis court* and *bowling green*, near St. Ann's church, and also an *archery*, and a *tennis court* in Gradwel-street.

THE POST OFFICE.

Is in Lord-street. It shuts every night at *nine*, for the dispatch of both the *north* and *south mails*. The *north mail** comes in every morning and goes out every night; the *south mail*, with a *coach*, comes in every morning, except Tuesday, about three (the *office* opens at eight) and goes out, as above, every night except Friday,

---

* Without a *coach* from hence, but joins the north mail coach to Lancaster, Carlisle, &c. at Preston.

and is 37 hours on the road each way, to and from London. The *York mail coach*, through Manchester, goes out every morning very early, and comes in every evening at seven; in one day.

The *mails* for Chester, North Wales and Ireland, cross the river. The office for these mails shuts every evening at six o'clock, from 5th April, till 10th October; and at four o'clock from 10th October, till 5th May.

The foreign mails are dispatched for Italy, Germany, and the north of Europe, every *Sunday* and *Wednesday*. – For Spain and Portugal, by way of Lisbon, every *Monday*. – For the Leeward Islands, the first and third *Wednesday* in the month: no postage required. – For Jamaica, the first *Wednesday* in the month: no postage required. – For North America, the first *Wednesday* in the month.

STAGE COACHES AND WAGGONS.

Are very numerous to all parts of the kingdom. They sometimes vary their *stations*, *times* and *fares*; so that every information respecting them, will be best obtained at the several *Inns*.

Liverpool Pottery

The economy of Liverpool has never been based on manufacturing industries, but on shipping, port facilities and commerce. However, in the eighteenth century there was a brief flowering of manufacturing in a specialised area – a considerable pottery industry – which acquired a widespread repute and made a very important technical improvement in the manufacture of ceramics.

There is inferential evidence of a pot making trade in Liverpool from the early days but no remains have been discovered which can be attributed with certainty. Products would have been made from local coarse clay and were probably mainly rough household utensils. There was a well established pot making trade at neighbouring Prescot and there is clear evidence of export through Liverpool in Tudor times.

The documentary record of potteries in Liverpool begins in 1714, when a lease was drawn up for Alderman Josiah Poole for an existing pottery, located at the junction of Whitechapel and Lord Street. The first dated and recorded piece of Liverpool pottery was made in 1716, probably at Shaw's pottery on Shaw's Brow. The so-called 'Crosby Plaque', was a large, landscape panorama of the village and district of Crosby. It was made in what is known as Delft ware, which emulated the Dutch blue and white ceramics. This type of ware remained one of the staple products of the Liverpool makers, who used it for a variety of ornamental and utilitarian pieces, ranging from apothecaries' jars to celebratory punch bowls. In addition, floor and fireplace tiles were a standard product of the Liverpool pot-banks.

John Sadler had an interest in both the printing and pottery trades and in 1756 he and his partner, Guy Green, were able to combine their expertise to invent the process of transfer printing on ceramics. This allowed cheap, colourful wares to be virtually mass-produced. The process was especially suitable for the making of tiles. On one

Herculaneum Pottery and South Shore

This print is taken from a painting by the most important Liverpool topographical artist of the nineteenth century, William Gavin Herdman. It shows the pottery established in 1795 by Richard Abbey at the Dingle, beyond the southern edge of the town. The ownership changed hands very quickly and the arrival of the potters from Burslem introduced a new style of products which often followed classical patterns inspired by the discoveries at Herculaneum – the name which was adopted by the pottery.

PHOTO: LEN FENDER.

occasion Sadler and Green, working alone, made 1,200 tiles in a day. Competitors were puzzled as to how a flat engraved copper plate could be applied to curved surfaces. In reality, Sadler and Green used the plate to print the design on paper which was then applied to the pot. Sadler made his fortune and retired to the country, his grave can be seen in the churchyard of St Helen's, Sefton. While transfer printing was being developed the Liverpool potter, Richard Chaffers, experimented with the manufacture of porcelain. He was successful in 1756 when he was able to locate a source of china clay in Cornwall.

The most famous of the Liverpool factories was established in the Toxteth area by a former apprentice of Sadler, Richard Abbey. He and a Scotsman, named Graham, took the lease of a disused copper works at the Dingle in 1795. After a year they sold the works to a firm, Worthington, Humble and Holland, who had plans for a major business development. The partners brought forty potters and their families from Burslem – they travelled by canal – to provide the nucleus of their workforce. Soon, the Herculaneum Pottery – so-called as a tribute to the discoveries being made at the excavations at the Roman city – acquired a national and international reputation. The pottery produced an infinite variety of wares: blue and white, brown printed, chocolate and ivory, with *bas-reliefs* in the Wedgwood style, street name plaques and figures similar in style to those of Staffordshire. The work of the factory can often be identified by a greenish tinge in the white colours, probably due to the use of copper waste in the glaze. The Herculaneum works passed through several hands until its eventual closure in 1841. Products of the Liverpool potteries are now highly prized and sought by collectors. One of the best collections can be seen in the National Museums on Merseyside.

MARKETS.

The Liverpool, like the London, markets are supplied from a very extended circuit. Northward, as far as Scotland, furnishes cattle and sheep; Ireland, a great quantity of cattle and pigs; and the Isle of Man and Wales, poultry, eggs, &c. The fertile Cheshire neighbourhood affords great quantities of vegetable and provisions of all kinds, which are brought over the river daily in the different ferry boats, particularly on the principal market days, which

are *Wednesday* and *Saturday*: the debarkation and embarkation
of which, at St. George's Dock slip, often present a busy and
entertaining spectacle. The great extent of sea coast pours in
various articles of consumption, including fish. Salmon is brought
fresh from Scotland and the north of Ireland, that taken in the
adjoining river, Dee, is the most esteemed, and is here called
Cheshire salmon.

The *fish market* is occasionally pretty well supplied, in the
different seasons, with *salmon, cod, flat-fish* (except *turbot*) and
crabs; shrimps, prawns, oysters, and other *shell fish,* (except *lobsters,*
which are always scarce and dear) very plentifully; *mackrel* and
fresh water fish are scarce; but *herrings* are mostly abundant. This
market, which is near the west end of St. George's church, is very
commodious; and where the *sisterhood* will be found to possess
as great a privilege and refinement of the *tongue,* as at any other
similar seminary. *Turtle,* on the arrival of West India ships, may
generally be purchased. It is commonly dressed at the inns for
distant conveyance.

MANUFACTURES.

The long established manufactures of the adjoining
neighbourhoods, have rendered any thing similar less necessary
here; and the minds of the inhabitants are more turned to the
exportation, than the *manufacture* of the different articles of
commerce. The principal manufactures, therefore, are chiefly
confined to what is necessary to the construction and equipment
of ships; the number of *shipwrights* only, is said to exceed 3000.

Copper plate printing upon earthen ware, originated here about
35 years ago, and remained some times a secret with the inventors,
Messrs Sadler and Green; the latter of whom still continues the
business in Harrington-street. It appears unaccountable how
uneven surfaces could receive impressions from copper plates. It
could not, however, long remain undiscovered, that the impression
from the plate is first taken upon paper, and from thence
communicated to the ware.

A manufacture of *Queen's-ware*, upon the plan of the Staffordshire potteries, has been lately established on the south shore of the river, about a mile above the town.

Here are several *mills*, of different constructions, for *cotton spinning*; and a great many *windmills*, for the grinding of corn, dying-woods, medicines, &c. Here are also several *sugar houses*; *tobacco* and *snuff manufactories*; *red* and *white herring houses*; two or three *iron founderies* and *pipe manufactories*; and a small *glass house*. *Glass* and *picture frame making* and *gilding*, have been greatly improved; and *printing* and *engraving* are in an advancing state; as also *coach* and *cabinet making. Watch making* has been extensively pursued; and Mr. Finney, an *artist* of the town, constructed a watch to be worn in a ring; which was presented to his present Majesty, many years ago.

The town is supplied with *ale* and *beer* from the public breweries, about forty in number; in general praise of which, much cannot be said. The indifferent quality of the *ale*, has lately been a means of introducing that necessary, native and wholesome beverage, from many parts of the surrounding country. An extensive *porter brewery*, in Scotland road, has been lately established; which promises to furnish as good a quality of liquor as the *London breweries*.

The Mercantile Elite

Business was the business of Liverpool in the eighteenth century. It was an environment in which the eager, the unscrupulous, the enterprising, the determined and the diligent could make their way to a fortune. In some cases, the new aristocracy of the town was drawn from families long established on Merseyside and they formed an elite which played a significant part in the affairs of Liverpool. The same names recur generation after generation, Clayton, Williamson, Norris, and Tarleton etc. These families intermarried and the complex web of interrelationships provided a real force in the government of the town. Membership of the charmed circle was a significant advantage in the prosecution of affairs. However, this oligarchy did not have an exclusive stranglehold on either the business or the governance of the town. It was perfectly possible for new men to make their way in the Liverpool world. Typical of this opportunism was William Boats. His peculiar surname was the result of the Poor Law authorities giving a name to a baby, found laid amongst the boats drawn up on the shore line, who grew to be a merchant and ship owner. On one occasion, after a particularly successful and cunning coup, he was seen dancing on the Pier Head and singing ' Billy Boats, Billy Boats, born a pauper, die a Lord!!'. He was never raised to the peerage but had a most successful career.

One of the most remarkable self-made men was Richard Watt, whose funerary monument is to be found in the parish Church of St Wilfrid, Standish, Wigan. Carved on it, as well as a portrait, is a remarkable relief of the Liverpool waterfront at the time of Watt's death in 1796. It clearly shows the Town Hall, George's Dock and the churches of St Nicholas and St Peter. Richard was born at Shevington, near Standish and in his teens went to Liverpool to seek his fortune. He was employed by an innkeeper, James Dimocke, to lead the horse which drew the only hackney carriage in the town. Dimocke evidently saw that there was more to the boy than fitted such a menial task and sent him to a night school to acquire literacy and business skills. His unchallenging work in the stables soon persuaded Richard to seek his fortune in a more exciting and exacting activity. Like many Liverpool youths, he went to sea. He did not return and all trace of him was lost but eventually merchants in Liverpool found themselves dealing in Jamaica with a firm of Richard Watt. Forty years after he left, Richard Watt returned to his adopted town an extremely wealthy man.

He remembered the days of his youth. He took great pains to trace members of the Dimocke family – two maiden sisters of his former employer – and provided them with a handsome pension of £100 per annum. Watt built himself a large house, named Oak Hill, at Old Swan and purchased from the Beauclerk family the decayed Old Hall at Speke, which he proceeded to restore and modernise. This property now belongs to the National Trust. On his death he left his heir, his nephew, above half a million pounds.

Another municipal benefactor who had been a migrant to Liverpool and left a permanent monument to his generosity was Richard Warbrick, who came from the eponymous village in the Fylde in the latter decades of the seventeenth century. He became a merchant in Liverpool and, at his death in 1706, left the sum of £120 for the building of an alms house for 'the widdow of some poor saylor of the Burrough'. Trustees, including the Mayor and the Rector, were appointed to administer this charity. Though Warbrick had provided for the building he made no provision for the maintenance of the widows. This was rectified by his nephew and heir, also Richard Warbrick, who left valuable lands to provide an income for the charity. It is of interest that the Warbrick Trustees – linked to another similar foundation of Mrs Ann Molyneux – are still an active body who pay an annual pension to widows and former seafarers. The Mayor and the Rector are ex-officio members of the board and the fund is still administered from the Parish Church of Our Lady and St Nicholas.

THE SCIENCES, POLITE ARTS, &c.

In a commercial situation, where all are constantly intent upon, and even immersed in business; the mind, if so inclined, has not leisure to detach itself from it necessary pursuits, so as to indulge in the more unprofitable study of the *sciences* or *polite arts*; the spare hours are, perhaps more properly, appropriated to such light recreations and amusements, as will unbend the mind and promote health. And if a man has had no opportunity of attaining an art of science himself, he is at a loss how properly to promote, or patronize it in others, although his wealth should fully enable him to do so: his habits and acquirements lead him to other pursuits, that may be equally beneficial to society. The *sciences* and *fine arts* are delicate exotics, that require a sequestered culture, and cannot be reared along with the general and more substantial harvest of the country.

A Library, in Lord-street, contains many valuable books for the use of the proprietors. It may be viewed, and any book examined upon the spot by a stranger. Here is no public *academy* or *seminary* for the instruction of youth or the amusement of mature age; which has always been the cause of an unfavourable reflection on the town; but, from the preceding observations, perhaps improperly.

Three weekly *Newspapers* are published, on different days, viz – Monday, *Billinge's Liverpool Advertiser* – Thursday, *Gore's General Advertiser* – Saturday, the *Liverpool Phenix* [*sic*] – wherein are detailed, the arrival and sailing of ships; the imports of the various cargoes; sales of imported goods; advertisements of outward bound freights, &c. these being the prevailing objects with the publishers, little regard is paid to the local incidents of the spot and neighbourhood, which might afford amusement if attended to.

The *Silversmiths* and *Jewellers* shops in Castle-street, &c. contain china, trinkets, and valuable curiosities both natural and artificial. At *Mr. Preston's*, in Castle-street, is an *artists repository*, for the sale of paintings, engravings, musical instruments, &c. There is a *music shop* in Lord-street, Paradise-street and Castle-street. *Booksellers*, *print*, *linen* and *woollen-drapers*, and most of the best *shops* for *wearing apparel*, are to be found in Castle-street, Pool-lane, Lord-street and Paradise-street.

William Roscoe, 1753–1831

William Roscoe was the most internationally celebrated inhabitant of Liverpool in the late eighteenth century. He was born the son of a tavern keeper, bowling green proprietor and market gardener, whose premises

Head of William Roscoe

This plaster profile bust, in the classical style, is modelled on the sculpted head and shoulders of the man, which was carved by William Spence, the foremost sculptor of the day. It is an indication of Roscoe's influence on the world of the period that a copy of this bust was given to Thomas Jefferson and can still be seen in Monticello, Virginia.

PHOTO. LEN FENDER.

were located on Mount Pleasant, then called Martindale Hill. Roscoe's poem, 'Mount Pleasant', written in his youth, depicts the rural tranquility of their life. William's schooling was at an establishment in Paradise Street, kept by a Mr Martin. At the age of twelve William voluntarily ended his education as Martin could teach him no more. He spent some time working on the family's garden – work which 'gave health and vigour to my body and amusement and instruction to my mind ... I considered to be the happiest of the human race ... those who cultivate the soil with their own hands'. However, he continued to read and study voraciously.

In 1766 William was employed briefly in a bookseller's shop but in 1769 he entered into articles with a lawyer and by 1774 had begun his own practice. In 1781 he was prosperous enough to marry Jane Griffies. The couple had a family of seven sons and three daughters.

Roscoe courted unpopularity in Liverpool when he spoke out against the slave trade. His work, *The Wrongs of Africa* (1787–1788) was a powerful polemic for the Abolitionists and he subsequently became one of William Wilberforce's closest associates. He continued to speak against the trade after his election as one of the Whig Members of Parliament for Liverpool in 1806.

Roscoe's horizons were not restricted to the Abolitionist cause or to his practice of law. He was a keen scholar and devoted much of his life to the collection of an unsurpassed library. He was especially absorbed by the study of the Italian Renaissance, and was inspired to write a *Life of Lorenzo da' Medici* (1796). The book won widespread acclaim and was translated into all the major European languages. It was at this time that he resolved to abandon his legal practice and to concentrate on his writing, on scholarly pursuits and from 1793 – inspired by his friend Coke of Norfolk – on the reclamation for agriculture of Chat Moss.

In 1800 he was forced to resume his business affairs. He became involved in attempts to save the bank owned by his friend, William Clark. At first, the venture was successful and Roscoe became a partner. In 1805 he published his second study of Renaissance Italy, the *Life and Pontificate of Leo the Tenth*. Though admired by some scholars, the book was generally considered inferior to his earlier work. Unfortunately, a new decline in the fortunes of the bank in the post war slump of 1816, found Roscoe facing arrest for debt. It was a measure of the esteem in which he was held that, when he raised funds by selling his library, many volumes were bought by his friends who returned them to him. Today they form part of the Athenaeum collection.

J.A. Picton in his *Memorials of Liverpool* writes 'It is remarkable how often we come across the name of Roscoe in connection with the most useful institutions of the town. The Athenaeum, the Botanic Garden, the Royal Institution, the Literary and Philosophic Society, the Academy of Art'. The Literary and Philosophical Society dates from 1784 and the Art Academy – in imitation of the Royal Academy was from the same period. The Athenaeum was founded for the encouragement of learning in 1797, the Royal Institution, 1799, was dedicated to the promotion of literature, science and the arts and the Botanic Garden opened in 1800 as both an educational and a scientific resource for Liverpool. This great man of Liverpool is commemorated by a garden on the site of the chapel he attended.

Matthew Gregson, 1748/9–1824

Any historian of the North West will, at some time, find it necessary to consult the 'Portfolio of Fragments Relative to the History and Antiquities of the County Palatine and Duchy of Lancaster' written by Matthew Gregson and published in 1817. Gregson, who was born in Whalley, lived most of his life in Liverpool devoting himself to his business as an upholsterer and interior decorator. His workshop was first at Castle Street and then, after the demolition of the building during the widening of the street, in Preeson's Row. Matthew Gregson married twice, in 1785, to Jane Foster by whom he had five children. His second wife, Anne Rimmer, was from Warrington and they had two sons and a number of daughters. Gregson was one of the new breed of Liverpool business men who were interested in the intellectual and cultural activities of the town. He was heavily involved in many of the same activities as Roscoe (the Liverpool Library, the Royal Institution, the Botanic Gardens and the Athenaeum). Like Roscoe, he was a keen advocate of local charities to which he gave lavishly. He was instrumental in the setting up of the School for the Blind and acted as treasurer to the Bluecoat Hospital. In this respect he can be seen as a colleague, or even rival, of William Roscoe, though their political outlook and fields of study were very different.

Gregson supported the attempted establishment of the Liverpool Academy of Arts and showed chalk sketches of furniture designs at their first public exhibition in 1774. While Roscoe studied the history of the Italian Renaissance, Gregson was most interested in the history and antiquities of his native area. He was an antiquarian rather than a connoisseur and dilettante. Roscoe was an abolitionist, a Whig and a reformer; Gregson was very much a supporter of the status quo and gave staunch support to the continuance of slavery. Matthew Gregson

THE ATHENÆUM,   RESIDENCE   DISPENSARY.
    1798.   OF G. CASE.

The Athenaeum and the Dispensary

This view shows the Athenaeum building on Church Street. Opened in 1797, in temporary accommodation, the institution was brought into existence to promote social facilities, to disseminate commercial and national news and to encourage learning. This new building, completed in 1798, to the design of John Foster, manifested these three aims in the provision of a news and coffee room and a fine library. The old building was demolished on the widening of Church Street in 1924 and a new club built in Church Alley to the design of Harold Dod. The doctors from the adjacent Dispensary – founded in 1778 to provide immediately available medical advice and medicines – were prominent amongst the founding members of the Athenaeum.

Dunbabin's Shoe Shop, Derby Square by Matthew Gregson

The shops of Liverpool were highly esteemed. Celia Fiennes and Daniel Defoe, together with other early visitors remark on the variety of commodities on sale in the shops. Unfortunately, few depictions of shops of the eighteenth century have been preserved. This sketch of the shop of Peter Dunbabin in Derby Square near St George's church gives a good impression of how they appeared. The windows are small and divided into many panes and typically the shop is raised above street level.

was infamous for his social climbing, and the world was astonished when he rejected a knighthood proffered by the Prince Regent when presented with a fine copy of the 'Fragments'. However, he was famed for his generosity and lavish entertainments, his house in St Anne's Street was often referred to as 'Gregson's Hotel' because of the number of visitors who could be found there.

He was a great patron of local artists and studiously employed local talent to provide the drawings and engravings in his books . He is said to have introduced the process of lithography to Liverpool with the intention of making drawings of local landmarks available to the public at low cost. William Hughes was responsible for many of the illustrations in the books and it was by Gregson's intervention and advocacy that he was appointed as engraver to the Prince Regent. Nor did Gregson despise the amateur and in the *Fragments* he included several illustrations by Rosamund White and others.

For a man so appreciative of artistic talent in others it is not surprising that he tried to develop his own skill at drawing, which seems to have been limited. However, because of the interest of the artist and the rather naive, but detailed, depiction of streets and buildings several of his own drawings are included amongst the illustrations of this book. As far as can be ascertained they have never been previously published.

Gregson's work was recognised by the world outside Liverpool. He was elected a Fellow of the Society of Antiquaries and of the Newcastle on Tyne Society. He became a member of the Society of Arts in 1801 and received the Gold Medal of that Society for his work on the reclamation of fire salvaged goods. The citation mentions that he had shown that paint, printers' ink and varnish could be manufactured from burnt grain. Gregson died at his house on 25 September 1824 after falling from his library ladder. His burial was at St Nicholas Church.

COMMERCE.

A minute detail of the *commerce* of Liverpool, would exceed the intention of this publication; but which may be obtained from the publication named at the third page. The trade of the port extends to every trading part of the world, the East Indies excepted; particularly to the West Indies, Africa, the Baltic, America, Spain, Portugal, the ports of the Mediterranean, and the north and south Whale-fisheries.

In the year 1792 an effort was made by the merchants to obtain a share of the East India trade, by a proposed application to Parliament. The situation of this country, with France, becoming more critical, and the derangement which soon took place in the commercial part of the kingdom, and of which Liverpool fully participated, suppressed the attempt.

The natural advantages, enumerated in the first page, which the port possesses, originally conspired to the formation of its commerce, and will always support and extend it. The staple commodities of coal and salt, are great inducements for ships of all nations to prefer a freight to Liverpool, as another is secured in return (partially or wholly, as other wares may offer) of these articles, so valuable and acceptable in every part of the world. The unrivalled cotton manufactures of this country, and the earthen wares of Staffordshire, can nowhere be shipped abroad to so great advantage as from here. The same may be said of the hard-wares of Sheffield. America takes off large quantities of all the above articles, and which are chiefly paid for with the money received for goods disposed of in France and the different parts of Europe. The ready communication with Dublin and the west coast of Ireland, must always ensure a considerable source of trade. The corn trade is very extensive; to which many of the largest and loftiest warehouses are chiefly appropriated; and which render Liverpool the granary of the interior country.

The town records state, that, in 1565, no more than 12 vessels belonged to this port, the whole of which amounted to no more than 175 tons, and manned by 75 men; the largest not exceeding 40 tons. The number of ships have always been in an annual progressive increase; so that in 1793 the number had increased to 606, of 96,694 tons.

It appears, that on the 24th June of the present year, 4,528 vessels had arrived in the course of the preceding twelve months; of which 680 were never here before.

In the late levy of seamen for the navy, the numbers were fixed upon the tunnage of the shipping in the different ports of the kingdom, and were as follow:

London	5,725
Liverpool	1,711
Newcastle	1,240
Hull	731
Whitehaven	700
Sunderland	696
Bristol	666
Whitby	573
Yarmouth	506

By estimates which have been made, assisted by EDWARDS'S History of the Colonies, and CHALMER'S Estimate of the comparative strength of Great Britain, it pretty conclusively appears; that Liverpool navigates *one-twelfth* part of all the shipping of Great Britain. That it has *one-fourth* part of the foreign trade of Great Britain. That it has *one-half* of the trade of the city of London. That it has *one-sixth* part of the general commerce of Great Britain. And that 606 ships belong to the port, whose burthen is 96,694 registered tons.

The *African trade* forms no inconsiderable part of the commerce of Liverpool. It appears* that, from the year 1783, to 1793, both included, the value of slaves imported into the West Indies in Liverpool vessels, amounts to 15,186,850l. sterling; 2,278,072l. being deducted from the above for commission and all contingences [*sic*] in the West Indies, the nett proceeds will be 12,908,823l. The Factor on remitting home the above, has a commission of 5 per cent. which amounts to 614,707l. leaving a balance of 12,294,116l. which on the average of the 11 years, is 1,117,647l. annually remitted; the clear annual profit of which, after deducting all other expences, will be to the merchant 214,677l. 15s. 1d. From this statement, the various manufactures and articles of commerce involved in the African trade, seems not readily calculable.

By estimates which have been made, it appears; that *one-fourth*, of the ships belonging to Liverpool are employed in the African trade; that it has *five-eights* of the African trade of Great Britain; and that it has *three-sevenths* of the African trade of Europe.

The Guinea Trade I

No description of Liverpool, in the latter part of the eighteenth century, can avoid a discussion of the Slave Trade or Guinea Trade, as it was usually referred to at the time. Dr Moss did not shirk the issue but tried to avoid giving offence to his readers. The trade now arouses such horror and creates so much opprobrium, that it is contentious to try to present it in the terms in which it was seen at the time.

---

* History of Liverpool, 8vo. page 223.

The situation is exacerbated by the accretion of myth, legend, misunderstanding and ignorance which have accumulated around it.

To the Abolitionist, the trade in human life was seen as appalling and degrading both to its victims and its exponents. There are few today who would challenge this attitude. This was not the case in the eighteenth century. The trade was fully legal and was seen as morally justifiable on the grounds that the black victims were less than men, that they lived in poverty under brutal and tyrannical leaders and that by transportation to the colonies they were introduced to the benefits of civilisation. As a consequence, their lives would be transformed, especially by their introduction to the Christian religion. As a result, they were saved from paganism and superstition. Today this argument is seen as nothing more than rank hypocrisy but we cannot assume that this was the case at the time. Views and attitudes change and it may be that in two hundred years time, opinions which are widely held and considered 'right' today, may be regarded with equal ridicule. It is equally unreasonable to attribute all the obloquy for slavery to the merchants and seamen of Liverpool. Liverpool was a latecomer to the trade. Slaving voyages had taken place from London and Bristol as early as 1564 when, despite the revulsion of Queen Elizabeth, John Hawkins made a profitable voyage from Guinea to the Spanish West Indian Islands. The early trade was sporadic but after the formation of the Royal Africa Company, in 1662, it developed apace, actively pursued by the merchants of London and Bristol in particular. The Treaty of Utrecht of 1713 granted the 'Assiento' – restricted permission for English ships to trade with Spanish America – which gave further stimulus to slaving voyages.

The first voyage of a slaver from the Mersey was that of the 'Liverpool Merchant' in 1700. In 1730 fifteen ships made the voyage. By the 1740s Liverpool had become a major player in the slave trade and rapidly outstripped the other ports. In 1744 more than half the English slave ships sailed from Liverpool. However, it is worth noting that even as late as 1804, on the eve of Abolition, 18 ships cleared from London and 3 from Bristol bound for the Guinea coast. In the time of Dr Moss it is calculated that Liverpool controlled 60% of the British slave trade which equalled 40% of the trade on a European wide basis.

The reasons for Liverpool's rapid acquisition of supremacy in the slave trade are a matter of dispute. In 1795, a writer suggested that it was due to the lower rates of pay and the more austere working conditions of the captain and crew of Liverpool ships compared to those of their nearest rivals, that allowed increased the profit margins. Probably more important to Liverpool's success was the availability from the port's hinterland of trade goods well-suited to the demands of the African rulers who provided the slaves. The light woollen and cotton textiles made in the Manchester and Lancashire area were more desirable than the heavy woollens of the West Country exported by Bristol. The coal and metal working industries of Lancashire produced items of hardware which were the second most important commodity used in the trade. The improved links by waterways to the potteries of Staffordshire, the metalworking centres of the Black Country and the gun makers of Birmingham added to the availability of useful, coveted, trade goods.

The Guinea Trade II

One of the enduring misunderstandings about Liverpool's participation in the Africa Trade is that the slaves were actually brought to the port. This was not the case in general, though there is evidence of the occasional presence and even sale of black men and women: these were exceptions. The legality of the ownership and sale of human beings in Britain was always dubious. After Lord Mansfield's judgement of 1772 in the case of James Somersett, slavery in Britain was declared illegal. The mechanics of the trade made it pointless to bring the victims to Liverpool, other than as fashionable house servants. The market for slaves was in the Plantations where they provided the essential work-force for cultivating the sugar, tobacco, cotton, and other crops. It was thought that the black slave could withstand the unhealthy climate, the harsh conditions and the intense manual labour which could not be sustained by Europeans. The supply of white convict and identured labour had proved unsatisfactory and it was African labour which replaced them.

The Liverpool Guineamen sailed for West Africa from the Mersey laden with trade goods in infinite variety. There were many destinations to which they made their way. All along the coast from Cape Blanco to the Congo there were trading posts. At these ports, the 'Factors' or agents had collected slaves, who were held in the 'Barracoons'. One of the most widespread myths of the trade is that the English sailors actually launched raids and captured their victims themselves. In fact, the slaves were rounded up by Arab traders or by other African chiefs who sold them, at a profit, to the factors or, in some cases, to individual captains. The part played by Africans in the slave trade was not restricted to a role as victims, many native kings enjoyed wealth and luxury from the sale of criminals, prisoners of war or those taken in deliberate raids. A contemporary note shows that in 1801 at Bonny, a single man slave was bought for trade goods worth £25. When one remembers that it is calculated that 303,737 slaves were carried on Liverpool ships alone during the decade from 1783 to 1793, the wealth being transferred into Africa was enormous.

Having bought their cargo, the ships headed for the unspeakable atrocities of the dreaded 'Middle Passage' and, in spite of the efforts of certain more humane captains, the horrors of this voyage can not be underestimated. In the Plantations of mainland America or of the West Indian Islands the cargo was sold and the return lading of tropical produce taken on board prior to the return voyage to Liverpool on the third leg of the infamous 'Triangle'.

As the Abolitonist cause gathered strength it was easy to make the Liverpool merchants and traders the scapegoats, and to cite the profits and prosperity of the town 'where every brick was cemented with black blood'. In fact, the slave trade was a vital plank in the economic structure of the country at large. The life of Georgian elegance and prosperity was based on slavery. Every man, woman or child who wore cotton clothing, smoked a pipe of tobacco, enjoyed the new drinks of coffee and chocolate, added sugar to their cooking or beverages was benefiting from slavery. The worker in the foundry at Backbarrow making cooking pots or the Furness farmer growing beans for slave provisions, a cabinet maker in the Gillow factory of Lancaster using imported mahogany to make furniture for a West Indian planter, was condoning and profiting from human misery. It was particularly unfair that Liverpool should have become the target of so much abuse and it is remarkable that it has remained ever since to embarrass the city and its authorities into gestures of apology. If such an apology is to be made meaningful it should be made by the whole of Europe, by the United States, and the countries of South America, by London and Bristol, Whitehaven and Lancaster and by the heirs of West African states.

The merits of this trade, in a moral and political light, have long been a subject of earnest contention by the legislature and individuals of this country. As a strictly moral question, considered in the abstract, it can meet with no countenance. In a political point of view, every thing favours it. That man, or body of men, would be wise indeed who could reconcile and assimilate two qualities so opposite and so much at variance in the human mind, as morality and policy; it is in vain to expect it, while man retains his fallen state. *Enthusiasm* may often be necessary in the *execution* of a great project, but never in the *projection* of it; which latter should always be under the guidance of deliberate reason, founded upon experience and an adequate knowledge of all the governing principles of the subject. And yet *enthusiasm* was the declared directing principle in the late attempts for the abolition of the trade, both in and out of Parliament. Can we suppose that the government, customs, habits and disposition of a race of people who cover a very considerable portion of the earth, can be made to undergo a sudden revolution at the *command* of a few who occupy but a distant speck, and thus invert the general order or nature by violent means? Not less ridiculous would be the attempt of the husbandman to shelter his crops from blights, storms and tempests, or to procure artificial sunshine in the absence of the great luminary, than any effort to wash the Blackamoor white. No doubt, projects to counteract the designs of providence, as extravagant as these, have frequently been nurtured in the mind of man, and have proved equally abortive. The system of human nature; whose process is hidden from man; cannot possibly be varied and directed by his will, who is ignorant of the great design; although he may be, and has been, made an accidental involuntary instrument, in ways undiscernible to him, in their execution.

Agreeably to the laws of nature, in the experience of the world, the attempt of the abolition of the slave trade was begun where it should have ended; and was like an attempt at bending the tree at its full growth, instead of doing it when a sapling; or purifying a stream at its foot, instead of its head; or curing a disease, without removing its cause: for, while the Africans continue in the same untutored, and consequently defenceless state, they must remain a prey to their more skilful neighbours – such *is* the character of man. Will the enlightened and refined European say, why his Creator doomed the mind of the African to remain as dark and naked as his body? He will acknowledge his ignorance; but must allow that it *necessarily* is so, hitherto; and that if he wishes to do him, what he supposes, an essential service in rendering him independent of his neighbour in future, it can only be done, humanly speaking, by informing his mind, and thereby instructing him in the usual means of self-defence.* As the condition of every situation, among mankind, is comparative; so the ignorance of the African slave makes him unconscious of being so; and hence, under proper treatment, his relative condition is much superior to many others, that might be pointed out, in all parts of the world. The thousand wants and cares of the *free* and opulent European, are unknown to him; the few he has, which his nature and education require, are gratified. Why then is his lot so very miserable?

The will of Providence being hidden from us, and since slavery has existed in all ages, and this particular part of it for a long time and to its present extent, instead of aiming to subdue it by violence, let us rather endeavour, as human prudence will suggest, to meliorate it to the utmost in our ability; and thus endeavour to palliate what it is not in our power to remove; in expectation of some crisis in its favour, similar to what all states and empires have so regularly experienced from the beginning of the world. Finally; in this, so extensive and complicated business, is it not better to act the part of *practical* rather than *speculative*

---

* Nothing can baffle human reasoning more, than the worse, if possible, than Egyptian darkness which pervades this quarter of the world: for notwithstanding the perpetual intercourse on its coasts with Europeans, such is the rooted ignorance, superstition and idolatry of the natives, that an instance never occurs of a native, on the spot, having any desire or being prevailed upon to receive any of the more enlightened instructions and opinions of Europe: and should a young native, after being educated in Europe, return back he will be considered as an impostor, and treated as such.

philosophers? The late decisions of the *legislature* seem to say so.
– Man cannot be influenced by any thing more inimical to his
natural happiness, than speculative philosophy.

Liverpool and the Abolition of Slavery

When writing his book, Moss found himself caught in a tangle of
views relative to the African trade. He was writing at a time when
the Abolitionist cause was gaining ground in the country at large but
was meeting with the fiercest opposition from the Corporation of
Liverpool. They opposed every move to alter the conditions under
which the trade was carried out and were adamantine in their resolve
that the total abolition of the trade was bound to destroy the
commerce and prosperity of the town. The Abolitionist cause dated
from the judgement of Lord Mansfield in 1772 and the agitation of
a number of Quakers who expounded the immorality of the trade.
The Anti-Slavery Society was founded in 1787. Its leadership under
Wilberforce, Clarkson, Sharp and other members of the Clapham
sect soon aroused public interest in the cause. Their efforts to obtain
legislation met with fierce opposition from Liverpool, whose delegates
lobbied the members of the Privy Council Committee and, when
legislation was proposed, the Members of Parliament. This intransigent
opposition continued until the eventual passing of the bill in 1807 which
made illegal the trading of slaves, though slavery itself was not illegal.
The vehemence of the efforts of the town to resist these changes
did much to blacken its reputation both at the time and subsequently,
when it became a target of condemnation from all sides.

However, even in Liverpool, there were prominent men, mainly
drawn from the Quaker and non-conformist groups, who were fervent
advocates of abolition. When the Society for the Abolition of the
Slave Trade was founded in 1787 a number of Liverpool merchants
became members. These included four Rathbones, a family whose
humanitarian influence was always pre-eminent in Liverpool and several
other prominent philanthropists, including William Roscoe. In 1787
Roscoe published the first part of his poem 'The Wrongs of Africa'
in which he delineated the horrors of the trade and predicted its
eventual eradication. In 1788 he produced a prose pamphlet entitled 'A
General View of the African Slave Trade'. This was immediately fiercely

challenged in a booklet, written by a rogue Jesuit, Fr Raymond Harris, citing biblical justification for slavery. Harris was rewarded for his efforts by a payment of £100 from the Corporation.

In the year when Moss wrote his *Guide*, James Cropper, a Quaker, became a partner in the firm of Rathbone, Benson and Co. and took on the fight against slavery. Over the next two decades Cropper developed economic arguments to show convincingly that by fiscal adjustment and the abolition of protective tariffs, sugar grown, using free labour in the East Indies, could successfully compete with imports from the West Indies. As a consequence, he predicted that slavery – which it had been expected would die after the abolition of the trade but was, in fact, flourishing in the colonies – would wither on the vine. To promulgate his views Cropper founded, in 1822, 'The Liverpool Society for the Amelioration and Gradual Abolition of Slavery'. At his instigation a similar organisation was created in London which both Wilberforce, Clarkson and a number of other prominent abolitionists joined. Though accused by his opponents of promoting his self-interest – his company were major importers of Asian sugars – Cropper abandoned the business to his sons and devoted his considerable energies to the cause. He travelled tirelessly on speaking engagements throughout the British Isles and also conducted a lively correspondence with the New York Society for Manumission and the Abolitionists of France. He gave £500 from his own pocket to Thomas Clarkson to act as a peripatetic speaker on behalf of the Society. It is an interesting contradiction of the prevailing view of Liverpool's attitude to slavery that Cropper received supportive petitions from the congregations of eight non-conformist chapels in Liverpool. Though his name is largely forgotten, Cropper was instrumental in the creation of a public opinion supportive of the Whig government's introduction, in 1833, of a parliamentary bill abolishing slavery throughout the territories of the British Empire.

BANKERS.

Messrs. ARTHUR HEYWOOD, SONS & Co. *Castle-street.* Messrs. W. CLARKE & SONS, corner of *Castle-street.* Messrs GREGSONS, PARKE & CLAY, *Lord-street.* The Banks are open from nine till three, every day except Friday, when they are shut at one.

AIR, SOIL, POPULATION, &c.

The following description of the state of the air, soil, water and other local peculiarities, are extracted from the *Familiar Medical Survey of Liverpool.*

"The situation of the town, as it effects the health of the inhabitants, has many natural and considerable advantages. From being situated upon the eastern bank of an open extended river, which has a near communication with the sea, the west side of the town is limited to, and confined in, nearly a straight uninterrupted line; by which its whole extent, on that side, becomes freely exposed to the fresh and unpolluted air of the sea, and an open country from the Cheshire shore: and as the westerly winds prevail a great part (nearly two-thirds, it is generally supposed) of the year, and that frequently in excess, the town is kept very regularly purified, ventilated, and freed from the lodgment and accumulation of vapours, and effluvia of various kinds, which, by retention, become highly deleterious, and unfavourable to mankind. The strong gusts of wind which come from the western quarter, so frequently throughout the year, are most singularly efficacious in these respects; and most especially so in the autumnal seasons; as they remove, or greatly abate, the bad effects which regularly ensue from summer's heat and continued calm weather, in large and crowded towns".

"If we examine the surrounding country, we shall find it every where, near at hand, free from morass, stagnant water, wood or any other cause or causes that can in any material degree conspire against, and are known to be unfriendly to the human constitution".

"The soil is sandy; which promotes the ready absorption, and, of course, prevents the stagnation, of rain and other waters; which contribute essentially to the health of the town".

"From the reason here assigned, the air of Liverpool must be, as it is, much more pure than it is commonly found in many parts of the kingdom; and which renders the town, in proportion to its size, much more healthful than most other large towns".

"'Notwithstanding the generally pure and healthful state of the air of Liverpool, it has, like every thing in nature, its occasional imperfections: the only, or principal of which are; its being subject to sudden and frequent variations in temperature, and being more than usually sharp and keen".

"In applying the foregoing considerations to the purpose of health, we shall find; that the situation of the town is, in general, very healthful; and that it is particularly favourable to constitutions that require and can bear a sharp, cold air; of which description are those of nervous relaxed habits, to whom in most instances, it proves very friendly and favourable: the healthy will also have their health preserved by it. The occasions in which the situation of the town becomes unfavourable, are with those persons who are subject to coughs, asthmas, and other affections of the breast and lungs, and are consumptive: as these are complaints that are aggravated and renewed, and even prompted in constitutions so inclined, by frequent irregularities in the temperature of the air, and its generally cold, sharp state".

The Water Supply of Liverpool

Dr Moss was unduly optimistic in his hopes for an improved water supply. For a hundred years proposals had been made which had come to nothing. It was to be another sixty years before a satisfactory scheme was achieved.

Liverpool had relied on water obtained from wells located in and around the town. The most important of these was the Fall Well, in St John's Lane. Water from the wells was carried by professional water carriers and sold to householders, or it was fetched by domestic servants. This was a time consuming and expensive business and often led to a search for wells in other locations. Sir Cleave Moore, in his rental of 1668, described sinking a well and reaching water at a depth of 14 yards. He claimed that the water was sweeter – many of the other wells were brackish – and softer than that obtained from other sources. It was especially good for brewing, laundry work and cooking 'pease'! Today, one of the urban wells is still visible in a shop in Bold Street.

Corporation Water Works – Berry Street

This pumping station dates from the implementation of the Improvement Act of 1768 by which the Corporation was granted powers to provide a water supply. The Corporation, in furtherance of this Act, issued a prospectus for a company to supply the town. Once the Company was established the Corporation renounced its interest, except in the name. The water was obtained from local springs and distributed through elm wood pipes. The original pumping station was in Hotham Street and the works in Berry Street marked the second phase of development.

PHOTO: LEN FENDER.

As the population of the town grew the supply of water became an urgent problem. In 1695, three London entrepreneurs proposed to provide water for the town, though they did not specify their source of supply. In return for an annual payment of £10 to the Corporation they were given leave to lay pipes, disrupt the streets and build a cistern. Nothing happened, except that the existence of their lease was to inhibit later schemes.

In 1705, Sir Cleave Moore, who owned land in Bootle which included a number of springs and streams of freshwater, proposed to construct an aqueduct to bring water into the town. Legal action was

taken to try to rescind the existing lease but, perhaps due to legal
difficulties or to a lack of capital, nothing was done. In 1718 Thomas
Steers was brought into the scheme but despite his business instincts
and initiative it remained moribund. Moore lost interest, sold his
estates in the Liverpool area and left the district. The scheme to tap
the Bootle springs was revived in 1721, 1748 and 1774 with different
developers but made no progress. By 1786 the Corporation, who
had until now largely neglected the development of civic amenities,
obtained the first Liverpool Improvement Act which gave them powers
for the repair and maintenance of the streets and for a water supply
plan under their supervision. The streets were paved and renovated
but the second provision was once more neglected. Perhaps the
disruption caused by the engineering works, which involved the building
of a pipe line or channel from Bootle and the laying of pipes in the
streets, was too daunting or the costs too great but, once more, no
work was actually carried out.

It was not until 1798 that another attempt was made to instigate
the works by the new proprietors of the Bootle springs which had
passed into the ownership of the Earl of Derby. It was opposed by
the Corporation who, for the first time, expressed an intention to
municipalise the water supply. However, they displayed little urgency
and it was not until January 1802 that a petition was placed before
Parliament and as a result the Liverpool and Harrington (a now
redundant name for Toxteth) Water Company was formed. This body
obtained its supplies from local wells and springs within the boundaries
of the town. In the same year a rival company, 'The Proprietors of the
Liverpool Waterworks', who drew their water from the Bootle springs,
was established. Despite its expressed interest the Corporation had
no financial stake in either of these companies. Even with two sources,
the water supply of Liverpool was 'intermittent, restricted and wholly
inadequate to the requirements of the town' . It was not until 1847
that a decision was made to create a whole new source of supply and
eminent engineers – including George Stephenson – were consulted.
The two companies were bought out by the Corporation prior to
the construction of a huge reservoir at Rivington in east Lancashire.
The new engineering works and pipeline construction was a major
undertaking and it was another 10 years before the water flowed into
Liverpool.

"As an addition to the natural purity of the air, we may add its being regularly, throughout the year, impregnated with the aromatic effluvia of tar and pitch, which are in constant circulation through the town; more especially when the wind is westerly; and which are well known to be remarkable correctors of the air, and particularly calculated to obviate and resist the power and progress of many infections diseases".

"The *water* with which the town is supplied for culinary purposes; and which is well-water, brought from the east side of the town; is unexceptionable in all respects; except the awkward mode of its being conveyed (in carts) to the inhabitants: being sufficiently soft and pure. The well-water which is obtained in the heart of the town, and near the river, is hard and brackish, and therefore never used for these purposes. This native purity of the water contributes a good deal to the health of the inhabitants."

It appears, from the above, that many local circumstances conspire to make Liverpool very healthful, and that the cooling refreshing breezes from the sea, in hot weather, render it a desirable retreat from the interior of the country at those seasons, aided by the salutary recreation of sea bathing. Such is the generally healthy state of the town, that infectious fevers are never known to prevail, and it is very rare to hear of a person dying of a fever of any sort. Agues are as rarely seen. There is yet another painful disease which seldom is heard of; and that is, the stone or gravel; which no doubt is to be essentially attributed to the softness and purity of the water. That disease being thus prevented; there can be no doubt that, when present, it may be removed or mitigated by the same means, and would well warrant a residence here for the purpose. It is proper to observe, that some of the springs are softer than others, and should be preferred. The best tests of the purity of water are, its being clear, and readily raising a strong lather with soap.

As the temperature of the air is so liable to be variable here, a stranger should guard against the effects of it, by an attention to the dress. The water of the adjacent sea coast is shallower than that of most others; which occasions the air that blows over it to be warmer here in summer and colder in winter, than on a coast where the sea is much deeper.

The most healthful situations in the town are the higher parts, beginning near the top of Duke-street and continuing the northern direction towards Mount Pleasant and Everton. The higher parts of the west side of town, bounded by Castle-street, where they are not particularly crowded with inhabitants, from being purified by the frequent westerly winds from the off the river, and the dry rocky foundation and sloping declivity, have always been healthful.

The following Table will give an idea of the increasing population of the town, from the earliest records to the present period.

In the year	Christened	Buried	Married
1660	3	0	0
1670	67	48	5
1680	106	51	3
1690	116	158	10
1700	132	124	35
1710	258	211	40
1720	410	293	53
1730	397	307	129
1740	485	608	137
1750	972	1075	290
1760	986	599	408
1770	1347	1562	433
1780	1709	1544	607
1795	2527	2009	753

The above statement will also give a view of the comparative healthfulness of Liverpool with other large towns, particularly London. In the latter, the deaths always considerably exceed the births; here, the reverse is generally the case; and when otherwise, it has arisen from a particular malignity in the small-pox or measles; the poor remaining inflexible in their opposition to inoculation; many of them from a motive contrary to preservation, especially among the idle and abandoned – a reflection not more melancholy than just.

The following is a statement of the proportionate annual mortality in different parts of Europe:

Vienna	1 in 19 ½
Edinburgh	1 – 20
London	1 – 20 ½
Amsterdam	1 – 22
Rome	1 – 22
Breslaw	1 – 26 ½
Berlin	1 – 16 ½
Manchester	1 – 25
Chester	1 – 31
Liverpool	1 – 27 ¼

The difficulty of obtaining these calculations with accuracy, for the purpose of comparative healthfulness, is very obvious. The inhabitants of some towns being much more prolific than those of others, and one-third of the children of large towns dying under two years old, with the different modes of living and employments, must greatly embarrass this kind of calculation. This town contains about 10,000 houses and 60,000 inhabitants; forming an average of six persons to one house. The town record states, that in 1565 it contained only 138 householders and cottagers, and consequently not more than 30 houses. The preceding tables will afford some idea of the increasing population of the town.

It has been observed in the first page, that this is the largest town in the kingdom, the metropolis excepted. The term *size*, is liable to a difference of construction. Some towns occupy more extent of surface than others, by the houses being more scattered, and being interspersed with gardens and other open ground. The

View of Liverpool from Everton,
Lithograph of painting by W. O. Herdman

The ridge at Everton still provides magnificent views over the city of Liverpool.
The essentially rural nature of the area in 1798 is emphasised in this picture.
Moss makes special reference in his text to the proliferation of windmills in
Liverpool. His explanation overlooks the fact that the wind was the most widely
used source of power on the whole of the west coast of Lancashire and this is
very clearly brought out in this view. Visible in this picture are three mills on
the north shore, a mill in Scotland Road, three others on Limekiln Lane, two
more at the summit of Shaw's Brow. Lime Street was lined with another three
towers and a further mill stood before the Workhouse on Brownlow Hill.

PHOTO: LEN FENDER.

declaration there made, arose from the number of men that were
levied for the navy by the last assessment on the *parish rates on
inhabited houses*. Liverpool, independent of Everton, Harrington,
&c. furnished *ninety-five*; a number which the reader will find to
exceed that of any other town, except the cities of London and
Westminster.

GENERAL OBSERVATIONS.

The great number of Wind-mills that surround the town, will attract the attention of the stranger as a singularity, with respect to numbers, not to be found in many other parts of the kingdom; the reason is, that most other large towns are of ancient origin, and were placed purposely on or near the banks of narrow fresh water rivers, adapted to the grinding of corn, and other useful purposes, and which are here wanting. Invention has attempted to supply the deficiency by a *tide-mill* which, however, has not been copied. As much water runs out of the docks at ebb tides, as would, if properly disposed, turn mills to grind corn sufficiently for the whole town, and leave water enough to wash the dock-guts.

Another singularity that engages the attention of the stranger, is the *Water-carts*, that supply the inhabitants with water for drinking, &c. It is said a plan is projecting to form reservoirs for the lodgment of water, by means of pumps worked by steam engines; the water to be afterwards distributed to the houses by pipes under ground. An act of Parliament was long ago obtained to bring a stream of water from Bootle (about three miles distance) which, fortunately was not executed, as the water, though clear, is *hard*, and consequently inferior to the water which the best town springs afford, which is remarkably pure, *soft* and wholesome.

The pavements of the foot paths of the streets, have of late been much improved; yet all strangers complain of their roughness and sharpness. The stones with which one of the side walks is laid in Castle-street, would be highly desirable in the other street: they are even superior to flags.

The streets are kept tolerably clean in general: yet a slovenly custom prevails, of suffering the dirt to remain in large heaps for some days after it is collected; which even the most wary will occasionally stumble into the night, in crossing the streets. This indecent practice has been attacked both by remonstrance and pleasantry; yet a *Hercules* is still wanting to cleanse the *Augean stable.*

The inhabitants of Liverpool have a more healthy appearance than those of most large towns; their employment being mostly of the active kinds, accompanied with exercise out of doors. This extends to all rank; and the pay of the mechanic and labourer is fully adequate to the temperate subsistence of themselves and families, for the preservation of their health. Inhabiting cellars, is extensively practised in some parts of the town. It has an unpleasant appearance; yet that is the worst of its qualities; a cellar being found, from experience, a much more healthful residence than a room in a house where every room is tenanted. Being detached, a cellar can neither receive nor communicate any thing infectious in the manner that necessarily happens in the inhabited rooms of a house that all communicate by one common stair-case; in which situation many families reside, who are unable to rent a whole house; and some entire streets are inhabited by tenants of that description. An order passed the Town-Council, for preventing the cellars being inhabited; but which was not executed – it might have pleased the eye, but would not have gratified the mind's reflection.

The streets and squares do not possess all the regularity and elegance that might be expected. The Builders, who were mostly born upon the spot, had no opportunities of improving their style, which was very limited; by which the streets, even the more modern, were laid out in the confined, parsimonious way that may be perceived; and that, even in situations which would have admitted more space, both in front and behind: a street was considered equally elegant, whether broad or narrow; and the houses equally commodious and valuable, whether they contained a depth of twenty yards or a hundred. This yet remains an error, not properly corrected.

The facility with which buildings are here constructed, has contributed essentially to the growing state of the town. Brick, stone, and sand for mortar, are all immediately at hand; and timber, from the Baltic, being directly imported here, is obtained at the cheapest rate. Lime-stone and slates are readily had, by water, from North Wales. Brick-buildings, which generally

prevail here, are erected with a ready dispatch; and they retain
their neatness longer than those of stone; which latter are sooner
discoloured by the smoke of a large town.

The stone here is soft when first taken out of the quarry, but
grows harder by exposure; and it retains its colour much better
than the Portland or many other kinds of stone, as may be
perceived by the Exchange and other public buildings.

Liverpool, from its sequestered situation, was not formerly
much the resort of strangers, for any other purpose than
commerce; and as the inhabitants were all embarked in business,
they necessarily formed a society among themselves, which, if not
refined by the grimace and ostentation of modern manners, was
proportionally uncontaminated by their influence. This commercial
intercourse of the inhabitants, induces a general harmony and
sociability, unclouded by those ceremonies and distinctions that
are met with in more polished life; hence the freedom and
animation which the town has always been observed to possess,
and which produces that medium or equality so rational, grateful
and desirable in society.

The wealth which of late has flowed into the town with its
extended commerce, has however introduced along with it some
of the more glaring luxuries of the times, which menace, by the
distinctions they create, the above boasted harmony of the whole.
A man in the middle walk of life, while embracing its comforts
and true elegances, will studiously avoid its ostentations, for his
own sake; as it invariably subjects him to many embarrassments.
The Spectator, finely observes; 'Men of sense have at all times
beheld with great deal of mirth this silly game that is playing over
their heads, and, by contracting their desires, enjoy all that secret
satisfaction which others are always in quest of. The truth is, this
ridiculous chace after imaginary pleasures cannot be sufficiently
exposed, as it is the great source of those evils which generally
undo a nation.' No. 574.

Liverpool – Another View

Ellen Weeton was born at Lancaster in 1776. Her father, captain of
a privateer, was killed in 1782 when serving in the American War.
In 1784 she moved with her mother and brother to Upholland near
Wigan. There, Ellen assisted with her mother's dame school until the
death of her parent in 1797. A period of hardship followed until, in
August 1808, Ellen decided to realise her assets and move to Liverpool
in search of companionship and a more active cultural life. Ellen was
a bitter, critical, outspoken, opinionated and censorious woman. It is
little wonder that she always found difficulty in retaining friends despite
her desperate correspondence. She soon alienated Miss Chorley of
Liverpool who had encouraged the move. After a short time living
with the Chorleys in Dale Street, Ellen moved into lodgings at Beacon's
Gutter, in Kirkdale. This was a '... very retired situation, but pleasant,
and clean without and quiet and comfortable within'. A lonely woman,
she found the company of the owner and the other guests enlivening,
particularly, 'the gentleman with a servant girl who took lodgings,
whose manner of conducting himself was not quite what I thought it
ought to be ... The gentleman occupied a two-bedded room; himself
in one and the servant – a pretty girl of 17 – the other; (but their
very great familiarity with one another during the day, made me, and
several others fear that one bed sufficed for both). The excuse he
made for requiring the girl to sleep in the same room was his ill state
of health, which required attendance several times in the night'. Ellen
enjoyed some aspects of the town 'I wish you could have ... seen
Mrs Siddons ... I went to see her as Lady Macbeth. We got very
comfortable seats in the gallery, and I was highly gratified. Much as I
expected, my expectations were exceeded; particularly in the scene
where Lady Macbeth is represented as walking in her sleep. The
whole audience seemed wonder struck.' But, on the whole, Liverpool
proved a disappointment. Her trenchant views of Liverpool do much
to contradict the euphoric picture of the sophisticated town painted by
Dr Moss.

'When I came to Liverpool I expected to have found it filled with
intelligent beings, imagining knowledge to be so generally diffused. I
begin to discover that it contains as much proportionate ignorance

as any little village in England, where perhaps the curate is the only intelligent man in it. How astonished am I daily to find so many more ignorant than myself, so few more knowing, considering as I have till now done, the great disparity of opportunities for acquiring knowledge between the inhabitants of so opulent a town as this, and the obscure individual of an obscure village, ... Here, not one in ten can speak their native language tolerably; not more than one in twenty, correctly; and of these last, scarce one tenth can boast any greater literary acquirement than that of their grammar. I thought myself very ignorant when I came here, expecting to find so many wise, so many learned – I find them not – I need not be very proud to imagine myself a little superior in intellectual acquirements to most of those I meet with – and how does it happen that I am so? The disadvantages I thought I laboured under in the obscurity of my rank, and more particularly in that of my situation, I begin to perceive were directly the reverse. It gave me so much leisure, that I had more time for the improvement of my mind than the generality of people here. Where there were no play-fellows, no toys, no amusements of any kind but such as I could find within myself, I had no other resource but reading and writing to fill up the solitary leisure. The people here do not seize the opportunities of improvement that so frequently occur – which they must almost wilfully reject – their ignorance is astonishing! It would almost appear as if ignorance was taught, as if it were something to boast of. Many intelligent tradesmen may be met in Liverpool, but generally speaking those of a similar rank in a little village are equally well-informed.' Perhaps Ellen was thinking of Mr Chorley – a tanner – who offended her and his daughter by indulging '... in a little perfume not such as costs him any money, nor such as is gifted with scent alone, but such as usher's itself into the world with some noise'.

The inhabitants are chiefly in three classes; the *merchant*, the *tradesman*, and the *labourer* or *working mechanic*. Men out of business rarely reside in the town; not even those who have acquired fortunes in it; who generally either mix in the gayer scenes of life, or retreat into the more retired.

It will be observed by the number of public institutions, that *charity* is a predominant feature of the town; where every call of distress is answered, and frequently anticipated. In addition to the public charities, the *necessitous* have a peculiar advantage. As nearly all the inferior orders are employed under the constant eye of the merchant; they are sure of his immediate indulgence, succour and protection in their various necessities; and are not suffered to exhaust their little stores, till the utmost distress forces them upon a public charity; the benefits, and means of access to which, they may have been ignorant of; and which in many instances, the modesty of their nature would lead them to avoid. This is a species of charity, that is not unprevalent; and is not more acceptable to the modest receiver, than grateful to the generous donor.

The police of the town is well preserved. A street assault and robbery is seldom or never heard of; nor is a burglary or other kind of house robbery ever attempted to any extent, by violence. Thefts of that kind are of a petty nature; as may be observed by the Sessions Calendar, quarterly. The nightly watch is well attended, and is doubled in the winter season, when it goes half-hourly; and the inhabitants are as secure in their beds as in the most retired village. The streets being in general well lighted with lamps, contributes much to the general security. Riots or tumultuous assemblies seldom occur, or are attended with any serious consequences.

A highway robbery, of any serious import, is rarely heard of in the neighbouring roads. Adventurers in that way have seldom succeeded; for as there are no lurking places for their security, and their retreat being cut off on one side by the river, the hue and cry, from the rarity of the occurrence, has always been so general as to ensure detection; even the town, from the vigilance of the police, will not afford a hiding place.

These securities from assault, may be considered as comforts not usually attendant on a large town. The *Mayor's Court* sits daily, within the Exchange, from eleven to three o'clock, for the purpose of regulating the order, decorum and police of the town. The *Sessions* are quarterly, for the trial of civil and criminal causes. The inflictions of the latter do not extend to death.

Local Government of Liverpool I

Since the granting of its charter (or, more correctly, Letters Patent) by King John in 1207, Liverpool had been a corporate borough administered by a Mayor, Aldermen and a Common Council of forty one members, representing the burgesses. 1795 was the centenary of the latest revision of civic government based on the Charter issued by King William III in 1695. This charter, which remained the basis of all Corporation activities, and subsequent charters, continued in use until the Municipal Corporations Act of 1835. The Mayor, Aldermen and Council were to remain as the central authority. There was a long standing dispute between the authority of the Common Council and the older system, by which the Corporation was to be chosen by the Common Hall i. e. a public meeting of the burgesses and freemen of the town. The 1695 charter left this matter still unresolved as no method of selection of the Common Council was specified and they were able to continue the existing system by which the Council was a self-selecting, self-regulating oligarchy. Efforts to increase democratic representation and a system of elections persisted. In 1790 one of the last attempts to make the Council elective had failed. As always, the Corporation was fiercely determined to protect its status and had the advantage of being *de facto* office holders while enjoying the blessing of unlimited money to fight their case.

The charter of 1695 brought about a change in the social structure of the Corporation. Until that date, it had been composed of men drawn from a variety of occupations and of various degrees of wealth and significance in the town. This charter shifted the balance to a small caucus of mercantile elite at the expense of the townspeople and the tradesmen. The new men, like the Johnson family, Richard Norris, and William Squire, were preoccupied with overseas trade, whether it was coal and salt to Ireland or tobacco from Virginia. Their main concern was the promotion of the new trades and overseas markets being reached by Liverpool ships. To this end, their main endeavour was with the development of port facilities – particularly the dock estate, and the creation of new income from the lands of the Corporation which were being rapidly covered with warehouses, factories and housing for the increasing population. Where earlier corporations had played a part in the life of the town and helped to meet its social requirements we can see, in the corporations of the eighteenth century, both a personal disengagement as the wealthy moved to new, salubrious suburbs and country estates in nearby villages; and an unwillingness, amounting to indifference, to the day to day running of the town.

To carry out its self-appointed tasks the Corporation had access to considerable financial and human resources. The income of the Corporation increased year on year. Dock dues, alone, rose from £810 in 1724 to £4,554 in 1771. Corporation posts were filled by 110 men. They ranged from 'dignitaries', such as the Mayor and the two bailiffs, the senior employed officers, for example, the recorder and the town clerk, down to those responsible for setting the stalls and scavenging in the market areas.

While the Corporation was directing its efforts to the development of the dock estate, the enhancement of river navigation, the regulation and collection of port dues, the management of its considerable real estate in the township and the surrounding areas, the encouragement of new trade and industries, to participating in and supporting improvements in the transport links of the town, to prestigious building projects such as the new Exchange and Town Hall, to the advancement and regulation of markets and trade, it was becoming more and more the keepers of the commercial destiny of the town, and less and less the governors of the whole community.

As they enjoyed the profits of trade, the Corporation failed to take account of the sixteen fold rise in population and all the attendant problems that the increase brought to the streets of the town.

Local Government of Liverpool II[*]

The Corporation was not the only body with power in the town. The Parish, or the Vestry, comprised the officers of the parish church together with representatives of the town elected at an annual meeting. It took responsibility for important aspects of social welfare and administration. It was the Parish who ran the Poor House and other forms of relief for the indigent. The Parish had authority to preserve law and order. The Parish had responsibility for the paving

---

[*]   I acknowledge the generous help of the late Dr Michael Power of the University of Liverpool with this section (D.B., 2007)..

To the PARISHIONERS of the Parish of LIVERPOOL

ANNUAL VESTRY

To be Held at the Old Church,
On TUESDAY next, at 11 o'Clock.

SEVEN YEARS Arrears of the
Poor's Rate laid on Shipping,
amounting to upwards of £.8000,
at present uncollected by the
Churchwardens.

Your Attendance is particularly requested at this Vestry, to support a Motion
for reducing the Parish Rates, and to resolve
that all Arrears of the Ship Tax be collected
with due Expedition, to make good such
Reduction, I am,

Your faithful and obedient Servant,

ROBERT CARR.

April 12th, 1800.

Printed by J. LANG, Fenwick Street.

Notification of a Vestry meeting April 1800

An idea of the scope of the work of the Vestry is provided by this poster.
This sheet is part of a series dealing with a deficit of £8000 in the
collection of the Poor Rate levied on shipping using the port which the
authorities had failed to collect. Though the implementation of the Poor
Law was one of the main concerns of the Vestry, the full text mentions
responsibility for the provision of the watch – twenty four additional
constables were provided by the Corporation after 1784 – street cleansing or
scavenging and paving.

and cleanliness of the streets. The Parish had responsibility for the repair and maintenance of the churches and their associated buildings. These obligations were met and paid for by the levying of 'Leys' or rates set by the Parish and collected by their officers. The eighteenth century Vestry was the heir to the various pieces of social legislation which mainly had their origins in the Tudor period. The officers of the Vestry were initially elected on an annual basis by the townspeople and were, at least in theory, volunteers for the posts. Liverpool as a single parish, faced great responsibilities and problems because of its large population. For example, the biggest undertaking of the Vestry was the administration of Poor Relief. It is calculated that paupers made up approximately 5% of the entire national population. On this basis, with a population of 5,000 in 1700, Liverpool had to deal with 250 paupers. One hundred years later, with a population calculated at 77,000, the number of the poor seeking relief would have been 3,900. Obviously, this implies a huge proportionate increase in costs. These charges had been, to some extent, offset by changes in payments of relief. Claims were discouraged by making the recipients wear a prominent badge on their clothing. The building of 36 dwellings for paupers adjacent to the Bluecoat School in 1722 enabled a reduction of relief payments to those who were housed there. The Workhouse, where the poor were expected to defray the costs of their keep by their labour, was opened in 1732. Under the direction of Joseph Brookes, the treasurer, a new purpose built Workhouse was provided in 1769. The building was extended in 1776, 1791 and in 1796 when it housed 1500 paupers and was reputed to be the largest such institution in the country.

In the face of the failure of the Corporation to deal with urban problems, the responsibility was undertaken by the Vestry. The fire engine, donated by Thomas Bootle, became a parish project. After serious riots in 1746, a ley was levied to support a local police force of constables under the parish constable. In 1778 the Vestry established a parish Dispensary, to which was added the provision of parish midwives in 1790 and the opening of fever wards attached to the Workhouse in 1801. Shortly after that it was the Vestry who became responsible for paving and lighting the streets.

To accomplish this work the Vestry found itself with an income of public money twice that of the Corporation. Initially, this was handled by a staff of seven amateur volunteers. Not surprisingly, the Vestry employed ever-increasing numbers of paid officials. In 1723 Edward

Crane was employed to act as Overseer of the Poor and a further six supplementary overseers were taken on. A full time Collector of the Poor Rate was appointed in 1726. Thomas Cockshutt, with an annual salary of 40 guineas, became the first professional Overseer of the Workhouse in 1734. Supervisors of the watch, of the paving of the streets, and staff of the Dispensary were appointed later in the century.

When the work of the Vestry in the administration of Liverpool is examined a sharp contrast with the efforts of the Corporation can be perceived. While the former sought solutions to the problems of the ordinary people, the latter, with greater authority and manpower, saw their main aim as the advancement of Liverpool as a port and trading place.

The *Government* of the town is vested in the Common Council, in the person of the Mayor, who is elected, annually, on St. Luke's day, the 18th of October, by the Burgesses. He has a personal allowance of 800l. a year for private contingencies.* The Corporation can make by-laws for the regulation of the town.

The greatest part of the town is leasehold under the body corporate, for three lives, and a farther term of twenty-one years, with a ground rent; the lives always replaceable under a fixed fine;† which, with the tolls or town dues, produce a growing revenue, at present of 25,000l. a-year. This was ascertained in 1793, when the Corporation stood forward to assist the merchants at that distressing period, by an application to Parliament to enable them to issue negotiable notes on the security of their estate; of the value of which, the following was the statement then produced.

---

* The Earls of Derby have frequently been Mayors of Liverpool. The last was the late Earl, in 1734.

† This *tenure* has its advantages. It greatly accommodates the transfer of property, which is done at an easy expence, and without any uncertainty with respect to title, &c. A tenant may change any life, under fifty years of age, as often as he pleases, for a guinea each, with the further expence of about 3l. for the new lease. When a life drops, it may be renewed at the charge of a year's rent, deducting one-fifth as a compensation for taxes and repairs.

General Account and Valuation of the Estate and Revenue belonging
to the Corporation of Liverpool, taken the 21ˢᵗ of March, 1793

Income for 1792	L.	s.	d.
Fines received for renewal of leases,	2,270	14	4
Ground rents received for 1792,	1,027	1	10
Rents for buildings in possession, let to tenants at will,	5,166	17	6
Rents for land in possession, let to ditto,	1,349	1	0
Amount of town's duties,	12,180	7	0
Graving docks,	1,701	16	5
Anchorage,	211	15	3
Small tolls called Ingates and Outgates,	321	9	7
Weighing machine,	143	4	0
Rents of seats in St George's church,	268	11	0
Arrears of interest from the parish of Liverpool,	360	0	0
	25,000	**17**	**11**
Interest and Annuities paid in 1792 Annual interest upon the bond debts, principally at 4½ per cent. per annum,	15,835	14	3
Annuities upon bond,	2,109	12	10
	17,945	**7**	**1**
Balance in favour of the Corporation,	**9,055**	**10**	**10**
Valuation of the above articles, adding that of land not built on, and the strand of the river,	1,044,776	0	0
Valuation of the debt,	367,816	12	0
Balance in favour of the Corporation,	**676,959**	**8**	**0**
Exclusive of a balance due from the trustees of the docks, and of the reversionary interest of certain lots of ground laid out for building, both together estimated at	60,000	0	0
Exclusive also of public buildings, and ground appropriated to public purposes, valued at	85,000	0	0

Liverpool is a very ancient *Borough*. It has ten Charters. The first was granted by King John, in 1203;* the last by George II in 1752. It sends two members to Parliament.

The calamity of *fire* is equally the lot of every town; depending upon circumstances, in the variation of the extent. Such is the quality of the brick, of which the houses here are built, that they are capable of resisting the power of fire to a considerable degree; so that when a fire happens in a house or warehouse, it is not liable to communicate to an adjoining house, under the assistance of fire engines.† A bell in placed in a central situation, to alarm the town in case of fire.

The decorum of the *Sabbath* is preserved in manner highly grateful to the feelings of every one who venerates it. The bustle of the preceding six days, settles in to a perfect quiescence in the seventh; an universal stillness prevails; and the various places of divine worship are well attended both morning and evening; when the public houses are shut; after which the superior families retire within themselves, while their domestics perambulate, in common with the middle and inferior orders, the town and environs at their pleasure, retiring peaceably at an early hour.

Liverpool has on all occasions been distinguished for its loyalty. At present, seven companies of foot, and a troop of horse, have regularly formed and accoutred themselves; and five hundred artillery men are enrolled, and have practised the exercise of the guns of the fort and other batteries, amounting to fifty pieces of ordnance, of 18 and 32 pounders; the whole of whom came forward voluntarily, without any expence to the public, for the protection of the town and port, if the regular troops should be wanted to act elsewhere.

---

*   This date is incorrect. The Charter was granted 28 Aug 1207 (D.B. 2007)
†   Here are three offices for Insurance from Fire, all well provided with engines, viz. Sun Fire, Royal Exchange and Phoenix Fire Offices.

Liverpool and Sea Bathing

Dr Moss was a fervent advocate of the use of sea water as a medical treatment. There had been a belief in efficacy of sea water in the treatment of numerous diseases for many years. In Lancashire, there was a tradition of visiting the seaside for therapeutic purposes at the spring tides, when 'There was physic in the sea'. Nicholas Blundell made a point of taking his young daughters to bathe when they were suffering from 'outbreaks'. In 1707 William Buchan's 'Domestic Medicine' advocated the practice. The freedom from restrictive clothing, the additional cleanliness and the sensual pleasures probably gave some benefits, even though they were largely psychological. In 1789 the physicians treating the first symptoms of his porphyria persuaded King George III to bathe at Weymouth. The fashion was set and places around the coast attempted to establish a bathing trade. In Liverpool it was the North Shore and the villages north of Liverpool that attracted most visitors. Sea bathing was established at Bootle, as Dr Moss describes, but also at Crosby Sea Bank, or, Waterloo as it became known. Later, in the nineteenth century, with the construction of the Liverpool–Southport Railway (1848) other coastal villages developed bathing facilities. A whole new resort was created at Southport from exiguous bathing arrangements which existed. A painting of 1830, by W. G. Herdman, shows the North Shore at Liverpool with numerous bathing machines on the sands and in the water, while the shore is scattered with picnic parties, shrimpers, children paddling and stalls selling refreshments. Near the sands is an old house owned by a family of Dutch origins named Van Dries who were the operators of the bathing machines. In the background several large ships can be seen passing down river. It is very reminiscent of one of the few descriptions we have of bathing at Liverpool.

In 1808 Ellen Weeton, a spinster from Upholland, moved to enjoy the bustling and sophisticated life of her Liverpool friends. She took lodgings with a family who let rooms to 'genteel visitors' at Beacon's Gutter, on the boundary with Kirkdale. Ellen delighted in watching the movements of ships and their occasional mishaps (a ship bound for Brazil was wrecked on the Black Rocks and its crew rescued by the locals. Much of its cargo of Irish linen found its way into the houses of the area). At another time she enjoyed a trip on the ferry boat to

Eastham, a popular destination for pleasure parties into the twentieth century. In summer time Kirkdale was invaded by bathers, some of whom were day trippers but others took lodgings for the duration of their stay. Ellen herself bathed, changing in the house and crossing the sands in her bathing dress. Such refinements were ignored by the majority who bathed in the nude '... the latter is not the most pleasant sight; but I am now accustomed to it, that really I do not feel so much shocked as I ought to do. It appears to me as a mere thing of course, and I think no more of the objects in the water, not notice them any more than I should passengers in the street'.

In addition to the pleasures of sea bathing, Liverpool offered other opportunities for bathing, which Ellen tried but found less stimulating, than a dip in the sea. The first baths were erected by a builder, named Wright, about 1750, on a site slightly to the north of George's Pier (Bath Street). They provided covered pools and a fenced, open air portion of the river. Their construction was speculative but Wright's outlay of £4,000 proved a profitable investment. The establishment was later bought and enlarged by the Corporation. Dr Moss describes the baths in his itinerary. They remained in use until 1816 when the building was cleared to make room for the new Marine Parade. A replacement was provided on the reclaimed land adjoining Mann Island. Upholders of propriety were reassured by the fact that, as Moss tells us, they 'were distinct for ladies and gentlemen and may be viewed'. In later years, we know baths of both hot and cold filtered sea water were available at a cost of 2s. 6d. Customers paid an annual subscription which ensured that only the genteel were admitted and social niceties preserved. In 1823 a proposal to enhance the amusements of the working class included the suggestion 'of a floating bath stationed opposite to the centre of the town. The Council had not been sufficiently continentalised ... the scheme was turned down'.

Liverpool from Bootle Bay lithograph

This lithograph emphasises the rural nature of the shoreline north of the town
and makes Moss's references to Bootle as a bathing resort more comprehensible.
Bootle Bay as a geographical entity has disappeared under the northern docks
built during the nineteenth and early twentieth centuries. The vessel unloading
in the foreground appears to be a 'Mersey Flat', the type of sailing barge which
carried cargo, especially coal, around the Lancashire coast.

THE ENVIRONS.

The following sketch of the environs of the town, is given as
a *guide* to the *stranger* who may wish to make excursions, to a
greater or lesser extent.

The *north shore* never fails being a pleasant ride, either in a
carriage or on horseback, in fine, warm weather; especially when
the wind is off the sea; as it is very refreshing, and free from dust.*
It will be adviseable keep close to the shore, or else pursue some
wheel tracks, to avoid the soft beds of clay that are interspersed, and
which may be discovered by their dark colour and uneven surfaces.

Immediately on passing the Fort, when the tide will permit,
will be discovered houses, with bathing machines, &c. which in
the season are filled with families, chiefly manufacturers from the

---

*   The *south shore* is impassable in this way.

interior. The rest are fishing houses, and the boats on the adjoining bank, fishing-boats. This part of the shore in the bathing season, is covered, at the times of high water, with such a promiscuous throng of sexes and ages in the water, as bids as great defiance to decency as it does to the calculation of numbers. To the credit of the town, it must be observed, that the inhabitants contribute very little to the spectacle, as it is chiefly composed of the description of persons just named. About a mile along the shore, a sandy road turns off, round a neat house with trees, and crossing the canal, leads to the village of Kirkdale; Walton being on the left, along the great north road; and St. Domingo and Everton in front, whence several pleasant roads branch into the country, to form pleasant rides.

About three miles along the shore are the Bootle mills (one a paper mill) and the two Coffee-houses, or Hotels, where genteel company resort for sea bathing and sea air, in the summer season. Here are public ordinaries, lodging and other permanent accommodations; and from hence a distinct view of the Rock Point and a favourable prospect of the sea may be obtained, as it discloses the track of ships to and from sea. The river at its entrance is so broad, that it has been conceived to resemble more an arm of the sea than a river. *Land-marks*, for directing the homeward-bound ships into the river, will be observed near this place. Adjoining, the *springs* arise that work one of the mills; and which were named as intended to be conveyed to Liverpool. The road from hence, after crossing the canal, leads to the village of Bootle, from whence, on the right, it proceeds to Kirkdale, lately mentioned. The straight direction, leads to Walton village and church; under which parish Liverpool once was subjected. This situation commands a good prospect. The church living, which is a *Rectory*, is a good one. All this is called *good*; yet a prospect of this kind is rarely pleasing, or highly grateful; since it is scarce possible to view it, in any direction, without contemplating the poor curacy in the back ground. Nothing personal is meant *here*; and from some late attempts in favour of the inferior clergy, their condition seems to be ameliorating.

This map is based on a survey carried out by William Yates, a prominent Liverpool cartographer, assisted by George Perry. The map emphasises the small size of the town and its generally rural surroundings. It shows the geographical relationships between the town of Liverpool and a number of places mentioned

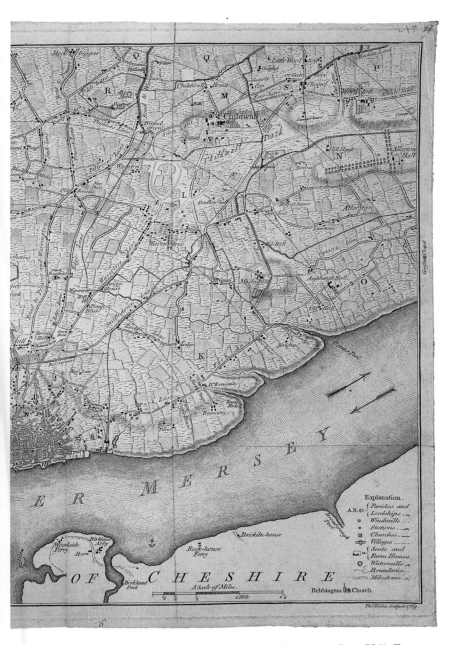

in the text. For example, to the north and east of the town Low Hill, Everton, Vernon Hall, Bank Hall, and Bootle can be located. To the south, the area of Toxteth and Wavertree can be seen. The ferry berths on the shore of the Wirral and various navigational aids are also marked.

Views of Everton

The development of Everton was one of the first examples of the flight of the
elite of Liverpool to more rural areas which were sufficiently near their place
of business to allow them to continue its supervision. The small hamlet with its
green and lock up became a favourite site for Georgian country residences; few
signs of these remain. The church of St George (1812–14) is a very interesting
example of the early constructional use of cast iron. The iron work was made by
Thomas Craggs at his foundry in the Dingle and the design was by
J. Gandy and Thomas Rickman. Rickman was a pioneer of the Gothic
revival of the nineteenth century and coined the terms for the categories of
medieval architecture (Early English, Decorated and Perpendicular) so
generally used today.

The left is the north road to Ormskirk; where originated the formerly celebrated, but now nearly exploded, medicine for the bite of the mad dog.* The right leads to Kirkdale and Liverpool. There is another pleasant road into the interior of the country.

About a mile beyond Bootle mills, along the shore and nearly in front, is the road to the village of *Crosby*, which may be discovered by the spire of the church; and about a mile from Crosby, is *Ince*, the residence of Mr. Blundell, where is a very fine selection of paintings, and of ancient statuary collected in Italy. They may, through the liberality of that gentleman, be viewed every Monday, by an order previously obtained. In the Temple, which is literally a Pantheon, that combines a Green House, we tread classic ground, in silent converse with original representatives of the deities of the heathen mythology – the effect is delightful. In addition to the rarities of this place, the owner's taste is displayed by an ornamental gate, which seems guarded by statues of a *lion* and *lioness*, of excellent sculpture. The whole is so disposed, that the lioness, upon the watch appears to descry an approaching intruder, and is warning the couchant shaggy monarch of it; whose adverted eye, towards his watchful mate, announces his attention to her signal. The *Hesperian fruit* could not have been more formidably guarded; and the fruit here is worthy such guard.

A few miles farther along the shore, is *Formby*, remarkable for the best *potatoes* in the county; in the quality of which vegetable, Lancashire is so well known to excel. It is known that potatoes were first introduced into England from Ireland; and tradition says, that a vessel from Ireland with potatoes to London was by stress of weather driven on shore at Formby (as sometimes happens) and by that means they became first planted there. It

---

* This famous medicine was made by Elizabeth Shackleton (née Parker) who had inherited the recipe from her first husband, a Cambridge-trained doctor, who had used it to great effect. After his death she took over the production and sold it at a modest 1 shilling (5p) per bottle and offered a mail order service. In 1776 she passed the recipe to her son but continued to make it herself until 1781. A Mr Hill of Ormskirk seems to have acted as her agent (see A. Vickery, *The Gentleman's Daughter* (Yale, 1998), p.254). (D.B., 2007)

House and coaches

This watercolour is the work of Matthew Gregson, and is dated 1775; the
place is not identified. It is an interesting depiction of one of the new and
fairly luxurious houses in the 'modern taste' which the wealthy merchants of
Liverpool were building on the rural fringes of the town. It gives illuminating
insights into travel at the time. The road is rough earth, dotted with stones and
cobbles. The wealthy can afford to keep their own carriage, in this case a chaise
with a postillion riding the offside horse. More usual and widely used for the
transport of goods were the pack ponies or here a mule seems to be indicated
carrying its panniers and driven by a pack 'wacker'. Gregson includes himself in
the picture, seated on the verge of the road with his sketch pad.

is very remarkable that this so very valuable a vegetable should
thus be cast upon the spot in England best calculated for its
cultivation – it may truly be esteemed providential. The tradition
receives strong support, from the culture of potatoes remaining
so long chiefly confined to this county and this particular part of
it. The real want of bread can never be felt while this charming,
wholesome and productive vegetable is freely cultivated. When of
flowery quality, it is found from experience to be better adapted
to a weak stomach, and to children and young persons, than
bread.

In a backward direction from hence, at a short distance, is *Sefton church*; observed by its spire, which, with the church discover elegant Gothic taste. The inside of the church possesses much of the grandeur of ancient workmanship; especially the choir, which contains sixteen ornamented stalls, and a formerly splendid canopy. The monuments here are chiefly of the Molyneux family; one of which is dated so far back as A.D. 1439. The following inscription on one of the tombs in the chancel, discloses the style and poetry of the time:

> Sir Richarde Molyneux Knighte & Dame Elenore
> his Wyffe whose Soules God pdon.
> Dame Worshope was my guide in life
> And did my doinges guide;
> Dame Wertue left me not alone
> When Soule from Bodye hyed.
> And thoughe that Deathe with dint of Darte
> Hath brought my Corps on Sleepe,
> The eternall God, my eternall Soule,
> Eternally doethe kepe.

Sefton is a valuable *Rectory*; where the same reflections that were made at Walton, at present more strikingly offer.

There is a road back through Litherland* to the shore, for a carriage, but which is sandy and heavy; and on the bank of the canal for a horse. The turnpike road adjoins; and which leads back to Liverpool. In approaching the town, the village of Everton, on the left, has a pleasing effect.

Two pleasant outlets offer through Everton towards the village of *Derby*; and beyond that to Knowsley,† the seat of the *Earl* of *Derby*, near *Prescot*, at eight miles distance from Liverpool. This ancient mansion remains distinguished by its images on the top,

---

* The Bowling Green at Litherland affords as charming a sea-prospect as can be well imagined, especially at high water.

† This is situated in West Derby, from whence the Earl derives his title, and not from the town of that name in Derbyshire.

The Well at Wavertree

This is a contemporary drawing of the well which attracted the attention of
Dr Moss. There are no reasons for his assumption of a monastic origin for the
canopy and its inscription, which look more of Georgian than medieval gothic
style. The well remains today and its appearance is little changed.

PHOTO: LEN FENDER.

its turrets, and ornamented chimnies. It contains an extensive
and valuable collection of paintings. The grounds, gardens, park,
&c. are on a large scale, and well disposed both by nature and
art. This extensive domain has of late been visited by its noble
possessor for a short annual period only; but which a recent
event promises to prolong; and which must prove acceptable to
a town and neighbourhood where the Countess's virtues and
accomplishments were so early known and respected.

The road back will be the turnpike; on each side of which are
interspersed several *villas*, chiefly the residences of the Liverpool
merchants, &c. One or two roads branch off on the left to the
villages of *Childwall* and *Woolton*, which are retired and pleasant,
and also lead to the town through *Wa'tree*.

View from Mossley Hill

This watercolour by a Thomas Chabband [?] probably dates from *c*. 1780 and is
from the collection of Matthew Gregson. Mossley Hill is now a busy suburb
on the south side of Liverpool but still bears some traces of its rural past. The
painting emphasises the agricultural landscape in which Liverpool was set in the
eighteenth century and what must have been the striking beauty of the Mersey
estuary. The highest of the Clwydian Mountains is Moel Famau and the absence
of the ruined Jubilee tower erected in 1810–12 to commemorate the golden jubilee
of King George III helps to date the picture. After 1794 the smoke from the pot-
banks of the Herculaneum pottery would have obscured much of the view.

A ride from the town, through the three last named villages, is
very pleasant. It begins by the *Wavertree* road (pronounced *Wa'tree*;
passing through that village, three miles from the town, in a
straight direction, a mile or two farther, to *Childwall*, pronounced
Childa. The sudden break upon the country, on entering
Childwall, has a wonderful effect; few inland prospects are more
extended and engaging. Parts of many different counties may be
seen from hence. Here is a *Coffee-house*, and a *bath* of remarkably

cold and pure spring water. A grave stone in the church yard, with initials, has a date of eleven hundred and odd numbers. – The right, and west, direction passes Childwall-hall, and leads to the village of *Woolton*, pronouced *Wooton*; where is a pleasant villa at the farther end, with a fine prospect. A comfortable dinner, &c. may be had at *Mrs. Denton's*; where from the bowling-green, the prospect may be advantageously enjoyed. The road backward, enters Wavetree nearly opposite the church. The good house to the left in front, upon an eminence, is *Mosley hill*; which displays elegance and chastity of design. – *Wavertree* is a pretty village, and pleasantly situated. It forms an agreeable contrast to the sea prospects nearer Liverpool. Here is a good Inn and Tavern, where regular *assemblies* are supported, in the summer season; composed of the neighbourhood, and company from the town. A *well*, near the pond, has the following singular inscription, of ancient date; which has been renewed.

Qui non dat quod habet,
Daemon infra ridet.
AD 1414.

It appears from this Monkish inscription, that alms were formerly solicited there; as it threatens the parched and thirsty visitor, who has any thing to give and does not give it, with the notice of a *demon* below, no doubt in the bottom of the well. An old monastic-looking house formerly stood in the scite of the modern adjoining one; and as this is the only spring in the immediate neighbourhood, it is not improbable that the house was inhabited by some religious order, who might thus extort alms towards their support. – The church, which is modern, is pleasantly situated, and its size corresponds with that of the village and neighbourhood. It has an organ; and the same neatness prevails within as without.

Toxteth park, forms an eminence on the south end of the town, at a mile distance. From thence a very good view of *Cheshire*, the *Welch mountains*, and the upper part of the *Mersey*, may be obtained;

as also part of the *Derbyshire hills*, or *English Appenines*, which
form a long chain of mountains in a north and south direction,
so as to constitute a middle boundary to the two coasts of the
kingdom. This district chiefly belongs to the *Earl* of *Sefton*; who has
an occasional residence, at *Croxteth*, in the neighbourhood. Some
attempts were offered to improve it by building, &c. but as they
were entrusted to his stewards, they were, of course, frustrated.

Bibliography

Ascott, Lewis and Power, *Liverpool 1600–1800* (Liverpool, 2006).

Belchem (ed.), *Liverpool 800* (Liverpool, 2006).

T. Bickerton, *Medical History of Liverpool* (Liverpool, 1936).

R. Brooke, *Liverpool as it Was, 1770–1800* (Liverpool, 1853; reprinted Liverpool, 2003).

K. Charlton, *James Cropper and Liverpool's Contribution to the Anti-slavery Movement*, THLC, vol. 123 (1971).

J. Davies, *Liverpool Studies 1795–1914*, THLC, vol. 153 (2004).

W. Enfield, *History of Liverpool* (Warrington, 1773).

S. Haggerty, *The Structure of Liverpool's Trading Community*, THLC, vol. 151 (2002).

E. Hall & J. J. Bagley, *Miss Weeton's Journal of a Governess* (Newton Abbot, 1969).

J.R. Hughes, *A Sketch of the origins and early history of the Liverpool Bluecoat Hospital*, THLC, vol. 11 (1858).

P. Hyland, *The Herculaneum Pottery* (Liverpool, 2006).

B. H. Lancaster, *Liverpool and her Potters* (Liverpool, 1936).

B. Lavery, *Nelson's Navy* (London, 1989).

D. Lewis, *The Churches of Liverpool* (Liverpool, 2001).

S. Nicholson (ed.), *The Changing Face of Liverpool 1207–1770*, reprinted Merseyside Archaeological Society (Liverpool, 2007)

E. Paget-Tomlinson, *Illustrated History of Canal and River Navigation* (Sheffield, 1993).

H. Peet, *The Liverpool Vestry Books* (Liverpool, 1915).

M. Power, *Creating a Port: Liverpool 1695–1715*, THLC, vol. 149 (2000), pp. 51–72.

J. A. Picton, *Liverpool Municipal Records* (Liverpool, 1883).

J. A. Picton, *Memorials of Liverpool* (London, 1875).

J. Rees, *History of the Liverpool Pilotage Service* (Southport, 1949).

Richardson et al, *Liverpool & Transatlantic Slavery* (Liverpool, 2006).

N. Ritchie-Noakes, *Liverpool's Historic Waterfront*, RCHM (1984).

J. Sharples, *Pevsner Architectural Guide* (Yale, 2004).

G.T. Shaw *Liverpool Homes of Mrs. Hemans*, THLC, vol. 48 (1896).

G.T. Shaw & J. Hughes *Birthplace of Mrs Hemans*, THLC, vol. 54 (1902).

M.M. Schofield, *Shoes and Ships and Sealing Wax*, THLC vol. 135 (1986).

J. Shepherd, *A History of the Liverpool Medical Institution* (Liverpool, 1979).

H.A. Taylor, *Matthew Gregson and the Pursuit of Taste*, THLC, vol. 110 (1958), pp. 157–76.

J. Touzeau, *Rise & Progress of Liverpool* (Liverpool, 1910).

Tyrer and Bagley (eds), *Nicholas Blundell's Diary*, Lancashire & Cheshire Records Society no. 112, vol. 2 (1970), p. 145.

H. Wallace, *A General and Descriptive History of the Ancient and Present State of Liverpool* (Liverpool, 1795).

T.S. Willan, *River Navigation in England 1600–1750* (London, 1964),

T.S. Willan, *Navigation of the River Weaver*, Chetham Soc., 3rd series (1951).

G. Williams, *Liverpool Privateers* (Liverpool, 2004).

A. Wilson, *The Cultural Identity of Liverpool 1790–1850: The Early Learned Societies*, THLC, vol. 147 (1998), pp. 55–80.

E·C· Woods, *Some History of the coastwise lights of Lancs. & Ches.*, THLC, vol. 96 (1944), vol. 92 (1945), vol. 98 (1946).

P.L. Woodworth, *Tide Tables*, THLC, vol. 151 (2002), pp. 19–51.

J. Vaughan, *The English Guide Book* (Newton Abbot, 1974).

A. Vickery, *The Gentleman's Daughter* (Yale, 1998).

Index